Secrets

A true Story from the other side of the Wall

Jane Roberts

WRITTEN WITH THE ASSISTANCE OF OWEN HUGHES

Imagine Records & Publishing International Inc.,
79, Chemin de l'Eglise
St-Sauveur, Quebec, Canada
J0R 1R0
FAX: 514 - 227 - 1937

Page Makeup
Owen Hughes

Cover Design
Alain Legoupil
Imagine Concepts

First Edition October 1995

Legal depot: Fourth Trimester 1995
National Library of Quebec
National Library of Canada

ISBN 2-9801966-8-1

Secrets

A true Story from the other side of the Wall

Jane Roberts

WRITTEN WITH THE ASSISTANCE OF OWEN HUGHES

I have seen black clouds and I have felt cold rain,
Now I want to stop and look beyond the pain.
The borders are gone and so are the fears,
So why am I crying a river of tears.
I guess it's just one of those moments in time,
Where you have to pack up and leave the past behind.
I said goodbye to a dream I believed to be mine
But which in fact fooled me with its perfect disguise.
Maybe that's why I'm feeling so sad;
Maybe that's why I still have to look back.
The System became my sanctuary, as I was taught,
Until it took my heart and tore it apart.
The Secret Land meant so much to me,
That I was lost when it turned its back on me.
Was it really as good as I thought
Or was it a failure of humanity as others declare.
Then the change came and rescued my heart;
I believed I was safe but couldn't deal with the scars.
It's time to understand and it's time to forgive,
Only then will I be ready to live.
My parents had surely intended no harm,
Even though they denied me a voice of my own.
They were captured themselves by the magic of trust
And the ruins of their dreams remain as the memory of their loss.
The sound of my voice now vibrates through the world
And there is no one to stop me from telling the tale.
This book and my songs are given to those who
Want to go on and who need to know.

Jane Roberts

First Words

Once upon a time, there were two children, a little girl and a little boy. They were born in Germany during the Second World War. After the war, when the country was split up, both of their families stayed in the eastern part. The late forties were tough years for many people all over Europe. The families of these two children lived in poverty and had to struggle for their daily survival. When the children became adults, they met for the first time. They decided to start a new and better life for themselves and their own future family.

The eastern part of Germany was directed by a socialist government. Over the years it became capable of providing people with basic human needs. Food, apartments and clothing were inexpensive. Daycare, kindergarten, school, college, university and medical care were all provided by the state. Everybody who wanted a job, had one. Nobody lived on the streets. Crime was unknown to most people. The country put a lot of effort into developing a peaceful consciousness within the new generation. They wanted to prevent another world war, especially one which might start again from within Germany.

The newly-married couple felt that this society was worth dedicating their lives to. They supported the system by working for thirty years for the Secret Service of the German Democratic Republic (GDR). Their commitment was so large that it touched every part of their life; the education of their children, the contacts they had with relatives and friends, the very way they viewed the world. The story of the system is parallel to the story of that family. There was no separation of work and private life, only constant control and commitment. Today, nearly five years after the fall of the Berlin wall, they find themselves alone, without friends, cut off from their relations and with a daughter who has taken the plane over the ocean to find a life of her own. That's me.

The memories of the Second World War still surround Germany like a dark shadow. The new generation resents the responsibility for this terrible war. They feel it is not fair to be born with guilt for history, just as it is not fair to be born with economic debts. At the age of twenty, my parents became young members of the Security organization and settled down in a village just a few minutes from Berlin. Geographically speaking, it is only a small distance from West to East but, in fact, it was as if I was raised on the other side of the world. My life in East Germany contained secrets which I was unable to share with anyone and which now form the substance of this book.

After being told for years that my path was set in concrete, it was tough and at the same time, very satisfying to learn that my life was suddenly in my own hands. To begin the process, I had to find out what it was I really wanted. In the course of my search, new avenues of possibility opened themselves up. One of them eventually led to my coming to Canada, something which I could not possibly have foreseen only a short time before.

After having decided I would go, I still had to make a choice between improving my life or staying trapped in the same old patterns. My first thought had been to just put the past behind me. I began to realize however, that no matter where I was, the pattern of the past would show up within a short period of time, even though it might hide for a little while behind new surroundings. I now know that I can't run from myself and I have found out that, anyway, there was never any reason to do so.

At first I did run, because I was afraid of what I might discover within me. I ran until I became aware that I had a right to make mistakes. From there I was able to develop and formulate my own very personal approach to life, despite the memories of a time when I had not been allowed to care about myself. After having been liberated from the chains of a society which imprisoned all individuality, all I wanted was to be true to myself. Now I am doing in Canada, what I began fighting for in Germany, to be able to write and perform songs.

This is the story of that journey.

Tegel Airport, Berlin, Germany

Am I really doing this? My hands are cold and humid. It's time to go to the gate. My heartbeat does not want to slow down. My parents and I look in each others' eyes and each time the question I see in theirs seems to become more urgent; don't you want to change your mind? I make certain to answer their look with a secure smile. At the same time I am quick to turn away, to find something else to look at. There is an expression on their faces that I haven't seen before, an expression of mixed sadness and helplessness. It just breaks my heart to see them this way.

There is some silent conversation; not much is spoken but so much is expressed. I am trying to comfort them by saying:

"Mama, Papa, don't worry, everything's going to be alright, I'm going to be fine."

My father just moves his head in agreement. Nor can he look me in the eye for very long. I have the feeling he just wants to run away, away to a place where everything would be as it was before. No strange, new society. No daughter taking the plane to another continent. No saying goodbye for who knows how long, maybe forever . . .

My parents have never seen anything beyond the Iron Curtain, never taken a big plane that could possibly end up crashing in the ocean. North America means little more to them than a spot on the map. Canada means nothing more than endless forests and pitiless cold winters. On top of this, it is a scary spot because it's so close to the United States which was, not long ago, the worst enemy of socialism and of their society. Now it is their baby who is flying away into this unknown, threatening world. So what else are they going to feel if not helplessness and sorrow?

My mom is trying to be positive. She expresses the hope that this will be the beginning of a good future for me. My father also tries to show some optimism but he is having a hard time. He is hugging my four year old son, Jan, over and over again. Now it's time to say goodbye. I am taller than my father so I am, more or less, taking him in my arms instead of him taking me in his. He begins to cry and I am so overwhelmed by his emotions that I have the hardest time fighting back my tears. For a moment I feel terribly guilty. I want to protect him by saying that there will be a reunion in the near future. Then I tell myself not to feel bad for my parents.

For the first time in my life, I am doing something just for myself. What a thing it would be if all my saved-up tears would come up just now. Here I am, the big girl, wanting to prove that I can do it on my own. My tears would wash away the hope they have that my decision is the right one. Their only comfort, if there is any, seems to lie in my Canadian boyfriend Pierre. I hope they are reassured by the confidence, determination and optimism we express together. Jan is walking around, curious but satisfied.

We take our bags and walk through the gate. From the plane I can see my parents standing at the window. They can see the take-off from there as well. My emotions are split. On the one hand I am excited, looking forward to the new life and on the other I wonder if it is right to be going so far away from my family. Inside I am fighting the same old fight: I am feeling responsible for my parents' emotions and experiencing the need to take care of my own. Here I go again, trying to finish this battle which my family has always fought, of each trying to live the life of the other. And even though this parting is painful at the moment, deep down I know it is for the best.

Bye, bye Mama and Papa.

March 1992, age 24

Although I am leaving Germany for good, it is not my first trip to Canada. It is now March but Pierre had invited me for the previous Christmas. The scene as we drive up to his house in the country is sweetly familiar. Snow is still on the ground and the forest is still an expanse of green and white, with the bare tops of the maple and birch shading it at intervals with a gentle grey. I love this forest scenery.

A few years ago in Germany, I was in a camp. I remember standing by a fence, looking at a huge tract of forest in the distance. The power of this natural scene touched my heart and I sensed a deep longing. Somehow I felt I belonged there. Now, looking at this beautiful Canadian scene, I am at peace again, in the same way. It is oddly like coming home. I am wondering how Jan is reacting to all this. He is staring wide-eyed at the country-side covered with snow. As we get nearer to our mountain destination, I say to him:

"This is our new home", and point with my arm at the scene around us. I am thinking:

"This is where our future lies . . . . doesn't it?"

Wismar, East Germany, mid-1970's

Every summer, when I was young, our family spent a three week vacation at a place called Wismar, close by the sea. Both sets of my grandparents lived there and it was there that my parents had met for the first time. My father's mother, who was Russian, died there in the nineteen fifties and my grandfather continued to live there until his death in 1980. Most of our ancestors came from Poland and Russia, except for my mother's mother who was of German origin. All of them were farmers who worked the land in that area.

My father's parents were able to make a living with their own little farm, while my mother's parents had to earn their keep by working on other people's land. Yet none of them were able to afford more than a poor life. My mother, who is an only child, grew up watching her parents get drunk, while my father grew up under the strict and often angry authority of his parents. None of their parents had received any special education and so they raised their kids in the simple way they knew.

When we went to Wismar, we always stayed at the

house of my mother's parents and visited my father's folks only once in a while. So this yearly vacation was about the only time that our grandparents got to see us. My mother has said lately, that really, I was not the first one to go so far away, when I went to Canada. It was just as far, in effect, for them to go to Wismar, because of the transport situation. My parents owned a Trabant, the most common car in East Germany. It was partly made out of cardboard and the waiting-time to receive one was from ten to fifteen years. Even if you had a car, the roads were not that good, so a voyage, especially to a place like Wismar, was not undertaken lightly.

I have some very nice memories of those Wismar days. One of them is of playing in the sand all day long, collecting shells and carrying jelly-fish around. How I used to scare my mother with those jelly-fish! We used to spend hours at the beach and never get tired of it. I loved stamping through the water that only reached my knees and didn't become deeper even a hundred meters out. I loved the feel of the soft sand under my feet, the smell of salty water, the fresh breeze and sunshine.

My sister Jana is five years younger than I am. When she was five, she was already a very pretty girl with lovely blonde hair. We loved to play in the water, on an air-mattress together. We had a lot of fun trying to stand up on it, laughing our insides out. Jana always had to leave the water early because she feels the cold quickly. Then my dad would get in the action. He and I would swim together on the air-mattress towards our destination: the waves. We would have the greatest time, smashing our mattress against the oncoming waves and letting ourselves be carried in by them. I needed to feel that my dad could enjoy spending time with me, just having fun. I can still see my father laughing in the water and I am laughing with him. I am proud of this moment of happiness shared with him. I am so proud, as if it was I who had accomplished something, just by making him laugh. I live for these moments.

We have to be like partners, choosing our favorite wave and then fighting it together in order to stay on the mattress. It's an incredible feeling of belonging together. I am saying to myself:

"See, Papa, how nice it can be with me. Now everything will be different. You will accept me now."

I believed this to be the beginning of a friendship and even though it didn't come true, I cherish these moments of pride and love in my memory. Maybe someday, there is still a chance my hope will become a reality. Now, my mind is going back to another scene, another kind of reality altogether.

On the way back to the house from the beach, my sister and I compare suntans and dispute as to who is the brownest. Grandma has already prepared dinner. The evening looks like it might continue to be bathed in the harmony of that holiday atmosphere. After such a day my mother and father are happy too. I can tell because my father is taking out his guitar. My father is a musician at heart. He can play the saxophone, the clarinet and the accordion as well as the guitar. It calms me to see how his usually severe face is becoming more relaxed while he is giving a little family concert. His tension seems gone, carried away by the sound of the music.

Now my mother and father are singing together. I love it. The voices of my parents sound really good in combination. Once in a while my mom has to stop because her cough is getting in the way. She suffers from chronic bronchitis, which is one reason she couldn't start on a professional singing career.

Once she told me that she had had a lot of ambition to sing and that people had told her in her youth that she had the stuff of a great singer. In her twenties she had stood on a stage to sing but the poor conditions of her childhood had left her with a chest condition, so she didn't pursue it very far.

As a little girl, she had to walk three kilometers to school. The winters back then were colder and the temperature in the north of Germany sometimes fell down to minus twenty degrees Celsius. Despite the cold, my mother only ever wore a jogging suit and she had no choice but to fight her way through the snow, freezing and brave. Conditions became even worse for her and her family when the only cow they possessed on their tiny farm, died and with it went a major source of nutrition. Of course, there was no money to get another one.

Having grown up in such poverty, it is now important to her to live in a solid way and she cherishes physical comfort. Still, her lifestyle is governed by a desire for simplicity because she believes it is good not to forget where she came from.

I am enjoying this peace and absorb as much of it as I possibly can. It feels like a relief, like a break from the feeling of being observed. Also, my grandparents are laughing and joking with each other. It is the peace that should never end. I wish it could be so.

Besides these beautiful memories, there are others. Memories that surround my childhood like the dark shapes of looming thunder storms. There is a grumbling from far-off but it slowly comes closer and closer until lightning hits the sky and is followed by the noise of a powerful discharge of energy.

The first days of our holidays are filled with excitement and happy tears at seeing each other again. As in every other year, one of my first activities is to go outside to see if the swing is still working. From out there, I can hear my parents' and grandparents' laughter and their loud voices. They seem to be speaking all at the same time. I am hoping that this happiness will be long-lasting. Longer than it used to be in previous years. I remember at least one angry moment during each of our vacations. And I cannot forget the way it happened or how it repeated itself.

I know the signs that announce the arrival of the thunderstorm. I am more than sorry to see that it is no different this time. After a few days, tension is in the air. Aggression is creeping like an enemy through the backdoor and our happiness starts to drift off into emotional turmoil. This is the time where my heart withdraws and hides deep inside of me. Here it cowers, hoping not to get hurt this time. But I feel my supplies of patience are getting smaller. I can't hold my breath much longer. I am not sure how to put it. I only wish for some peace or forgiveness regarding my existence. Or . . . maybe I will explode.

Yet, it's not an explosion which takes place. That will come later. The longer I repress my pain, the more it gets converted into a different shape, that of rebellion. The time of terror is near. It is indicated when my father gets up in the morning in a bad mood. He hates to be in a bad mood, he can't stand himself in one. It seems as if he is afraid of being discovered, afraid that someone might inadvertently see the open wounds in his heart. Left untreated and ignored over the years, they have turned into something like hatred. At the same time, it seemed to go hand in hand with a sort of helpless vulnerability. What a painful mixture. I got to feel it. He often nagged about my bad moods. Was he frustrated about seeing me go the same road and yet being, at the same time, the one leading me there? I think Father was trying to rid himself of the madness by distributing it to those around him.

Holy Moley! These are my words sixteen years later. Back then I felt worthless. The only use that I felt I could make of myself was to become the 'brat of the century'. I did not really plan this, it just more or less happened. I remember now . . .

I am waking up. It is a beautiful summer morning. The sun is shining through the window and birds are giving me their morning concert. The wind is rustling in the trees. I can hear bees passing by the window. They seem in a hurry this morning because they go vimmmm, vimmmm all the time, faster than usual. In Grandma's house I don't need a clock. Every morning I am woken up by flies sitting on my nose. I don't know why flies like so much to sit on a person's nose. Maybe it's because, from a fly's standpoint, the view is better.

While I'm scratching my nose, hiding under the blanket to have a few more undisturbed moments, I start to be conscious of the sounds from the kitchen downstairs. My father is at the wash-basin in the kitchen, shaving his beard. I can hear his voice. Its range tells me what kind of mood he is in. It is low and scratchy this morning. From the sound I can also tell that there is no smile on his lips as he talks. These are bad signs.

My attention is drawn away from the nice summer-holiday morning as I try to feel out the situation down-stairs. My anxiety about the moment where my father might get mad, is rising. I start to make out the words. My father is nagging about things. Nobody else says anything. I know what that means. I am trying to think out a strategy in order not to get into trouble with him when I go down. I am afraid to be the one causing an explosion of anger again.

Maybe I should make myself invisible, not go near him, so that he doesn't realize I'm there. Or, if it's impossible to be overlooked I should be as sweet as possible. I also consider the idea of behaving totally normally, as if everything was o.k. That means I pre-tend to be deaf and blind but even behaving normally doesn't help. Father's pressure has to escalate in order for things to be fine again. I know that from numerous previous experiences in the life of my family. And besides, even if I pretended everything was ok, my father knows that it isn't. So he'd make sure to create trouble until everybody else knew that something was wrong.

I am fearfully expecting my father to utter a certain phrase. This foreknowledge gives me a piercing feel-ing in the belly. I know each time I have that feeling, I am close to saying something to my father which I shouldn't. Something that only brats say to their par-ents. I don't know how to stop it. It is like a mecha-nism I can't control. Each time I prepare myself, telling myself that I will not be touched by his comments. Yet each time my father finds sentences that somehow drive me up the wall. I feel provoked, aggressed and insulted. Now my anxiety drives me out of bed.

Suddenly I hear my name. My heart beats faster. Coming downstairs to the kitchen I can feel the bad vibes that are threatening our peace. He receives me with a cool:

"Good Morning, Pina. It's time you got up! But you look very morose, didn't you sleep enough after all these hours?" He is deliberately trying not to talk too loudly. The vibration in his voice tells me that he too is nervous. Anger is boiling inside of him. I carefully reply that I have slept enough. I am already beginning to shake a little inside. I hear him say:

"If you slept enough, then put on a more friendly face." Anxiety strikes me and I don't really know where to turn or what to say.

My mother helps me out by offering me some breakfast. It's my favorite meal, white bread with butter and strawberry jam and milk. For a time, nothing more is said.

My father is still at the wash basin. It's the only source of water in the house. He's been there for an hour, shaving his beard with annoying thoroughness. There is no toilet or shower in the house. Outside there is a little cabin with a toilet.

Father criticizes. There always seems to be something wrong. Whether his shaver is not working properly, the coffee not strong enough, the floor too dirty, my Grandma talking too 'stupid', my Mama too slow in handing clean socks and underwear or me standing too often in his way, there is always something. Things are not perfect; few things seem to deserve my father's approval. Everybody around here is busy trying to keep him happy. It is obviously our responsibility not to upset our father, husband or son-in-law.

I know this kind of situation. It is like a mechanism which repeats itself. I know what's at the end of it. The final blow will come down on my head. I know if I get away today he'll get me tomorrow. These are desperate days of trying to escape from trouble. I have the impression that when my father has no reason to get mad at me, he creates one. He puts a lot of effort into trying to make me react. He is always observing me, commenting on the wrongness of my words. Each of my sentences is analyzed, searched through for a weak point. Out of the blue he sometimes gets back to a sentence of mine which I used hours ago. He seems to choose harmless phrases on small subjects. He disputes my words and gets angry over them. He wants me to listen and to agree to everything he says. If I don't he calls me stubborn and tells me I am condemned to failure. I feel squeezed and have no space to breathe.

Once in a while my mother tells my father to leave me alone. He tells her to shut up. Sometimes I am able to deal for quite some time with this pressure. While the pressure is growing, his frustration is increasing too. It makes me endlessly sad and in the long run I am sure it will drive me crazy. It happens regularly but I live in the hope that on a given day, he will not get mad at me. I try hard to be a better person but I don't really know how I am supposed to do that. I feel guilty about being the cause of so much criticism.

My mother sometimes says that these vacations are too stressful for her. Instead of relaxing she has to make sure that things are 'right'. Her function as a diplomat is hard to endure because there is no willingness from father's side to make things easier. In that regard he has little respect for his family or himself. He is suffering through all this too. While he is terrorizing us, his anger is not getting resolved, merely loaded with new fuel for the fire. Is he angry about ruining the harmony which existed just a short time before?

It is amazing how fast Father can switch from aggressivity to sweetness or the other way around. He is like a yo-yo that jumps up and down. We have to jump with him.

On another evening, my parents and grandparents were sitting at the table. I didn't understand the whole of what was talked about but the subject was familiar to me: politics. Any kind of conversation can lead to that. The talk can begin with cars or just about anything else. My father always manages to draw the line of argument towards politics. I don't recall any talks we had between father and daughter. All I can remember are lessons given by a politician to a student. During those so-called conversations, I was judged in advance to be an unwilling protege.

That particular evening I was watching TV. The adults were talking in the kitchen and drinking alcohol. Their talk slowly drifted into a dispute. My father raised his voice. My grandfather tried to forestall him:

“Pssst, we can talk normal”. My father went on:

“No, listen to me...” and started his noisy explanation again. An argument was in the making. I heard my mother say:

“Oh no, not again. Leave it alone! Can’t you talk about something else than politics? That is impossible to endure.”

My grandmother added a comment, agreeing. My father shouted at her:

“Mind your own business! You don’t understand anything of this anyway, stupid as you are”. My grandmother was revolted. My mother instructed my father to watch his words. He scowled but did not reply. Then my mom said to Grandma:

“Come, let’s leave them alone. It doesn’t make sense to get excited over that. Let the men shave each others’ heads if they want to.” My father was especially angry that night and it looked as if the big explosion was going to occur. My mom and Grandma withdrew from the scene. They came into the living room and I asked them:

“What, is Father arguing politics again?!”

My mom put her finger on her mouth, warning me not to speak too loudly. If Father had heard my question, he would have jumped on me. For my sister and I, it was time to get ready for bed. Fortunately for Jana, she was too little to follow any of that but I am sure the tension radiating in the house did not completely spare her.

It seemed my father had heard my comment after all. He suddenly shouted:

"What is she nagging about again!" My mom said:

"Nothing."

My father kept stressing some point he wanted to make. In doing so, he got more aggressive. He yelled and his fist hit the table several times. My heart jumped up and down. I heard my name again. I started to cry because I knew my dignity was going to be crushed again. My father was shouting:

"Pina is worth nothing. Always when it comes to learning something, she closes her ears. She does not want to hear the truth."

My mother rushed into the kitchen:

"It's enough now, leave her alone. She did not say anything."

My father started yelling at her:

"Shut up. Stop interrupting me all the time. Not one more word. I can't say anything in this goddamned stable of a house." My mom told him to stop. He screamed even more and threatened to hit her if she said another word.

My mom came back to my room. I was lying on my bed, crying. She sat by me and caressed my face. Grandma came in too, shaking her head at the madness of my father. In the kitchen, my father screamed out loud:

"People want to understand nothing. They are all lazy and want everything to be done for them. Pina is one of them. If her whole generation is like this our society is not going to get anywhere. It is all going downhill because of people like her. The only thing she is capable of is nagging."

I began to whine:

"*Ich hab' doch gar nichts gemacht. Ich bin lieb, ich bin ein liebes Mädchen. Ich versteh' nicht.*"

"I didn't do anything bad. I am good, I am a good girl. I don't understand." My mom softly replied:

"I know. Go to sleep now."

I asked her why dad always got so mad at me. She said:

"I don't know." I asked her:

"Doesn't he love me?"

"Yes, he loves you."

At that point my mom started crying:

"Never think that your father doesn't love you."

I had a hard time understanding why it was then, that he could get so furious with me. In those moments, it was as though I was receiving nothing but hate from him. Where was the madness coming from? Was it from me? My mom told me to try to sleep. She left the room and went back to the kitchen. My father had finally calmed down. I heard her say to him:

“You don’t know what you are doing to Pina. One day this will have a bad ending. You will see only much later the damage you are doing here. This is not good for her health.”

The next day everything seemed to be ok. My father had rid himself of his pressure. Life went on and I was happy that it was over for at least a few days. The next time he shouted at me, he added to his destructive repertoire that I was responsible for the disharmony in our family. This went on for years and his frightening speech became the basis of my beliefs. This is where my self-confidence never had a chance to develop and the remains of it became rotten through lack of nourishment.

A few days later we went to the port in a city nearby. We were walking on the docks. I don’t know what I was feeling but for some reason I covered my eyes with my hands and stepped backwards towards the water. I was coming closer and closer to the abyss that went down five meters before reaching the water. My father wasn’t around for a few minutes. Even though I was terribly scared, I kept on moving backwards, without knowing how far I was from the drop. Something inside of me pulled me towards the water. My mother was terrified to see what I was doing. She didn’t call after me because with one more step, I would have fallen in the water. She took the camera and told me she wanted to take a picture. This is how she managed to stop me.

After that my fear of falling was too strong and I moved away.

Poland 1945

The streets are burning. Buildings disappear in flames and smoke. The bombardment is finished and has left a burning chaos for the survivors. People come out of the basements to face a brutal reality. A mother is holding her two little children tightly by the hands. Together they are trying to get away from this nightmare. They are stumbling, climbing terrified over dead bodies that cover the street. One of the two children is about three years old. He is my father.

This scene is one of his earliest childhood memories. He was traumatized like millions of others by the happenings of the Second World War. The war which had started from Germany eventually returned there, bringing what had been sent out: death and destruction. After almost two years of going East, through Poland towards Russia, the Germans were stopped by the Russian army around St Petersburg. After mobilizing all their available forces, the Russians initiated a movement which proved to be the turning point of the war. The Germans could get no further than Moscow, beaten like Napoleon, by the cold.

For the first time, the Germans had to face the possibility of defeat. Once the Russians had pushed the Germans out of their own country, they decided to keep pushing them on through Poland. Soon an even bigger power struggle was taking place, involving the world's heavyweights - Russia, America, France and England. It became a question of who was going to win the control over Germany and its potentially enormous economic power.

As the fighting moved through Poland, thousands of people were swept towards the West, away from the battle front. The closer the fighting came to the German border, the more the streams of fugitives swelled. The fear of revenge from the Russians made those who fled leave everything behind.

My father was born in the middle of the war, in Poland. He already had three older brothers. His mother was expecting twins but only one of the two made it through. My father remembers being blamed by his mother for having taken too much space in her belly, so that the other twin had no room to live. The little boy never forgot the heartless statement. Neither could he free himself of the sadness he felt because of that. Besides that he had to spend his early childhood years under the brutal fact of the war. Many of our mothers and fathers carry wounds of that war in their hearts.

Trying to escape from the fighting in Poland, my father's family packed what they were able to carry and caught a train filled with hundreds of other fugitives. At one point the train stopped and it was not clear for how long it would remain idle. My father went with his older brother to get some water for the family. They had to walk some distance because there was no water close to the train. When they returned with the water, the train started moving. Screaming, they start to run. Anxious and fearful to be separated from the family, they reached the train with the last of their strength.

The family moved towards the north-west of Germany, close to the sea. They settled down in the little village of Wismar, where they found a place to live. The war came to an end but poverty was rife. The Russians still moved West while the Americans came from the other side, moving East. When the armies met the war was finally, really finished. The Germans were defeated and peace had been achieved. The point where the armies met became the border between East and West Germany. My father's family was in the territory that the Russians had reached. Later on, it became known simply as East Germany.

The majority of the people were very afraid of the Russians. When their army finally moved into the cities and villages with their trucks and armor-plated vehicles, people remained in hiding. What a surprise it was when they suddenly settled down in the middle of the street and started to erect portable military kitchens. They started cooking soup and noodles and winked to people to come and join them to eat. They were carefully observed by the hidden crowds. Scared but curious, they watched the Russians at work. Desperate and with hungry eyes, they looked at the way the Russians were cooking the meals that the people had missed for such a long time.

One of the children who looked on was my father. Finally, hunger won over fear. People began to slowly come forward to receive a warm meal. At first they came one by one and then more and more people walked forward. Their faces still showed mistrust and disbelief at this act of generosity from the 'enemy'. Yet the rush of getting food into their stomachs made them give up their doubts. My father went forward with the rest, to get something to eat. He says he cannot forget that moment, when he was given a bowl of spaghetti. It influenced his whole life. He was filled with gratitude for the generous act of the victors. It had come to him as a little boy in a moment of great need. At this point his heart became indisputably connected to both the Russians and their spaghetti. He still adores noodles today. Noodles as a code for well being and Russian soldiers as a code for peace.

When my father talked about some of his painful memories, he always finished by saying that was why he gave his heart to the most humane of societies and that he goes on in his life in spite of the pain he has known. In his eyes, ours was the best possible society because it could guarantee what he had not had as a child. He wanted people to understand that they had to be patient, that they had to take one step at a time. He believed that the society was in the process of slowly improving everybody's life together and he could not understand it when people criticized.

Frankfurt (Oder), East Germany, 1970's

My parents lived the positive example of what they were working to achieve at the social level. They spent their entire GDR life in a cramped three room apartment, without so much as a small garden to extend their living space. They accepted the minimum, thinking that everybody had to be raised to that level before improvements could be made in their standard of living.

We moved to that apartment when I was five. Although it was centrally heated and we no longer had to use coal, my mother always said she preferred the one we had left outside of Berlin. There had been less traffic and the block was surrounded by trees. Still, in the new place we had a telephone which not many people had at that time.

Soon after we had settled in, my sister arrived on the scene. I remember going to the hospital with Papa. I brought my little triola on which I had learned a song with Papa's help. I was so proud to be able to play that song for my Mama in the park in front of the hospital. They both applauded me and for a minute I enjoyed having their full attention. I wanted to play the song over again but Mama and Papa wanted to talk to each other and wouldn't let me. I felt rejected then and today, when I find myself in a similar situation with my son, I try to remember how important it could be just to pay attention at a particular moment.

Later, we sat in the car to go home and I remember watching that tiny face with little white pimples all over it. That was of more than ordinary interest to me and I followed every move she made with keen eyes.

Soon after Jana was born, I started school. It was the beginning of my real initiation into the mysteries of socialism, the force which would so influence my life for nearly two decades to come.

Friedensschule, Frankfurt (Oder), 1974

In 1974, at the age of six, I had my first day at school in Frankfurt (Oder). My school was called Friedensschule, the School of Peace. All the schools had names like that. All of us, parents and children alike, were welcomed to the school in a big hall. There were about forty children to be placed in two groups. One child after another was called to the front and welcomed to the class. I became more and more impatient, asking myself when I would finally hear my name. As the last name was called before mine, I felt sad to be the only one left but relieved that the wait was over.

Yet my name did not come up. I sat there in disbelief. I could see my parents were getting nervous. What had happened? The teachers were beginning to form the children up in lines to go out of the hall. People nearby looked at us, realizing that there was a problem. I sat glued to my chair, waiting for something to happen.

My parents explained that I belonged in one of the groups but the director could not find my name on the list. I heard some adults expressing their sympathy about it - it was quite a special occasion. The teachers of the two groups were about to leave the hall to walk to the school when I started to cry. I felt angry about the pity of the others because all I wanted was not to be forgotten. After a discussion between my parents and the director, we went outside to join the others who were already on their way.

I had come to my first day at school in a festive mood, dressed up nicely and curious about what was to come. Now I found myself running with my parents to catch up with the others, as though I didn't quite belong. I asked myself why this had to happen to me. It was not an auspicious start to my school career.

In all the class rooms, school buildings, daycares, offices, streets and shopping centers we would see pictures of our leaders, especially the former president, Erich Honecker. Along roads and inside college buildings, signs were put up that said:

'*Everything for the good of our people!*',

'*Forward to the next party congress with the best results!*',

'*Everything for peace, friendship and socialism!*',

'*Words and actions have to be a unit!*'

Having been exposed to these pictures from early childhood, they seemed perfectly natural. We didn't know anything else. We grew into this one and only truth from the day we were born. Socialism was given to us with our mother's milk .

Yet there were some people who did not want to identify themselves too completely with this new society. During the one-party, socialist regime, they had no political power, yet they provided an undercurrent of discontent. So there were two truths in that world, the public and the private, the official and the unofficial.

There was only one kind of school for everybody so we were all mixed up together. Children who had parents working for the Secret Service were brought up at home in a strict socialist environment. Out of twenty students in our class, six of us had parents working for Security. The Security organization was also known as the Stasi, to people on the outside. Compared to us, the other kids were exposed to far less political dogma. As Security kids, we developed a different point of view about the society. This automatically caused a certain tension at school. In our school system, we spent ten years in the same class with the same people. Since the underlying differences in our backgrounds were so profound, it was extremely difficult to develop healthy, normal relationships.

The others were allowed access to western channels on radio and TV and some of their families had contacts with relatives in West Germany. The kids would come to school singing the latest advertising jingles they'd heard. There were no advertisements on the eastern media, so it was a subtle form of one-upmanship to know these tunes. All of this was forbidden by both the system and our parents. It was a big disadvantage socially, to be left out.

The western world was known for the glamour and commercialism which was attached to everything, including school materials. Products from the Eastern-bloc countries were simple, without any effort made to shine or to catch the attention. Security kids could not have those much-desired articles that other children would show off with, in school.

Officially, any western products such as T-shirts, were forbidden in public places. It was so in school also, but in the groups, the kids would always manage to show each other some smaller western articles, such as bubble gum with little stickers. It was the yardstick of peer-group respect and integration. The more you could show your connection to the West, the more 'in' you were.

From a young age we learned about this 'double life' in our society. While many kids spoke with the proper tone during lessons and social occasions, they acted differently in private. What was said in one place was sometimes the exact opposite of what was said in another. Circumstances like these kept the doors closed to open communication. In class, the scene would be like this. During a political discussion, someone would venture the opinion that our system was very efficient in some way or other. Immediately, hands would start to shoot up as others joined in the automatic giving of praise for all things socialist. The thing was just to show that you agreed.

For me, the vocabulary always remained the same. I believed the same thing whether I was at home or at school. Even my childhood games reflected my adherence to the system. One day when I was about seven, I came home from school feeling very bored. I decided I was going to make a little celebration to mark the military success of my parents.

I knew where all their distinctions were stored and,

feeling totally enthusiastic, I started to take out all the medals, tokens and deeds that they had received over the years and put them in fine order on the dinner table. Every family owned a flag that was put out only on national holidays. Ours was a red one which is the symbol of the blood of the working class. I went to get it and in a solemn manner, I dragged it out to the balcony where I put it in the metal flagholder for everyone to see. Then I found some military music and, turning the volume up very high, I opened the balcony door as wide as I could.

Satisfied with my preparations, I sat examining each of the various distinctions very closely. The Security building was just across the street. Some people working in the offices opposite our window, knowing that this was my parents' apartment, informed my father that the red flag had been hoisted on his balcony. In disbelief he looked out the window and saw that it was true.

A sudden sound at the door interrupted my happy celebration and my father soon stood before me in the living room. When he saw how I had decorated the table with all the medals, he started to laugh out loud. He could not stop laughing as I explained to him what I was doing. He took me in his arms and convinced me to put the flag back in the closet. I knew my parents would like my party for them. For years after it was a popular episode to repeat to relatives and friends.

Another, similar event occurred a year after that. Every once in a while, it was common to collect small amounts of money from the pupils in school for Solidarity purposes. The money was of course given to us by our parents. The evening before the day on which we were supposed to bring this contribution, I saw my mother arranging the budget and distributing money on the table. As I watched the little piles growing, I suddenly had the urge to give more than the five marks which we normally allowed. I thought there was enough on the table so that it would be appropriate to take some more with me to school.

Even though I knew that my parents supported the idea of Solidarity premiums, I had the feeling they would not give me one of those nice bills if I asked for it. As I did not want it for myself, I justified the theft by saying it would be for a good cause. At a moment when my mother left the room, I sneaked to the table and put a beautiful red-colored bill in my pocket. I wasn't too sure what I had done and I went out of the room with a pounding heart.

The idea of being a great help to poor people in the world and the thought of being admired for my largess, were stronger than my bad conscience. After all, I reasoned, my parents didn't really need it because there was still plenty left. Nobody would even know that there was something missing. Nor did my mother notice at once. She only knew when she got a call the next day from my teacher who wanted to verify if she was aware that I had brought a fifty Deutschmark bill to school.

When my mother carefully asked me if I had taken any money from the table, I could no longer hold back the secret. Fortunately, I wasn't blamed too much. The explanation of my parents that it was not decent to take things away like that, was eased by their amusement with my desperate act of solidarity. I remember my father joking how little Pina meant to make things easy by simply adding a zero to make it fifty marks instead of five.

From first to third grade, everybody joined the organization called the Young Pioneers. Those who wanted to be part of it and not attract the attention of the system, would naturally join in. I remember the mother of one child who did not allow her son to become a member. As a result he was excluded from the activities of the class after school. In order not to expose children to that kind of rejection, they were usually made to become members. The Young Pioneers wore blue scarves and white shirts on special occasions.

From the fourth to the seventh grade, the blue scarves were exchanged for red ones. In the eighth grade we became members of the Free German Youth and wore blue shirts showing a rising sun on a badge. It was a constant process which kept us where the system wanted us. Everything was planned and all we had to do was to follow the path.

The older we got the more extreme and contrary the kids' opinions became. At official functions, most people put their blue shirts on at the last possible moment and had them off again as the last words were being spoken. That was the cool thing to do. Only the Security kids who were taught to love the system at home and at school, remained constant to it.

As we reached the teenage years, this became a real problem for our little group. The division was becoming more marked. On the one hand we were all thrown together yet on the other we were taught to have a distanced attitude towards people who were not involved with the Security branch. It was a tough row to hoe.

We started having political arguments in the group. A struggle started about which society was the best one. The other kids accused our gang of wearing pink glasses and being unable to see without them. The kids would get mad whenever one of us would talk about the system. The arguments became more and more belligerent and the group, which had never been a cohesive one, split further down political lines.

For me, the worst nightmare of a teenager was not to belong to the clan. We were both afraid and ashamed of being outsiders and angry at not being understood. Some of the Security children tried to keep the peace and stopped defending socialism. Maybe they were the smart ones since they got away from the emotional damage.

I remained totally convinced that my society was on the right path and I would not hear any criticism of it. Besides, this is exactly what I was being warned about by my parents: not to be receptive to negative comments. I considered the arguments of the kids as attempts to get me off the path. It disturbed me deeply that they were not as convinced as I was. I could not understand what was wrong with guaranteed social security, guaranteed jobs, an entirely free system of education, working for peace instead of war and cherishing the family. I could not follow why others praised the western system so much, as I knew about unemployment, social insecurity, high living costs, high crime rate and homeless people.

The non-Security children had different information coming to them through the western media. I only believed what my parents told me and what I could read in the newspapers. My father's heart belonged to the political struggle and my heart belonged to the family. That's why politics became such a part of me at such a young age.

I remember how toughly I defended my family, when some children insisted that my parents watched western TV. I told them, No! They don't! I could not accept it as a possibility. I thought I knew better.

Eventually I became curious about what was being shown on these forbidden channels and I dared to put one on myself. Between my heart pounding and listening for the door, it was all I could do to concentrate on the movie. It was showing all those Jewish people trying to escape from the hell in Germany during the war. They were trying to get to America.

As I sat there enthralled, I heard the door bang and realized that it was too late to change channels. Before my father could understand what it was all about, I was crying in his arms, saying I would never do it again. He seemed to be so shaken by my behavior that he did not think to blame me. I was so happy and started to tell him that the movie was not talking against our system at all. It was even supporting our teachings by showing a story about the bad Nazis.

I was very moved by this discovery. I had been afraid of the western media as if it was the pure incarnation of evil. I had been taught that it would divert us away from our political mission. I asked my father for permission to watch western television. Of course I didn't get it but what I didn't know then was, that both my father and the system he supported were afraid of the same thing: that people might find out the whole truth about the West.

A little while after that, one of the Security kids openly admitted that he watched western TV. He was in charge of political development in our class. What he told us immediately earned him more respect from the group as a whole. I was both surprised and impressed with his news. I said to myself, if he can do that, maybe I can do it too.

I confronted my parents with what I had heard. They told me that it was out of the question for me to watch western television. Their argument was that this boy was far enough ahead not to let himself be manipulated and would be able to tell the difference between right and wrong. I was hurt by that statement because it clearly meant that I could not be trusted. I could scarcely believe that that could apply to me, since I was always manifesting the very essence of the socialist credo. I began to wonder what was going on.

In school, the tension between the two factions mounted. The teasing from the others escalated until it became a daily routine. The boy who had started to watch the western channels was no longer a target so the harshest verbal attacks were directed at me and came mostly from other boys. As a girl, I was doubly attractive to them since my political strictness precluded any soft relationships from developing. In my mind I saw only the need to live for my country and I believed I had no need for a boyfriend.

I had a hard time dealing with being picked on every day. About this time, I started to feel ashamed of who I was but was nonetheless too proud to give in. I got into verbal confrontations and tried to hide my hurt and fear behind a front of arrogance. Yet I was deeply insecure because I could not catch up with the current knowledge about western music or fashion. It meant, at some level, that I was not acceptable. I was not trustworthy either.

My mother's notion about bringing up her daughters was that they should be very modest. She rarely bought herself a new piece of clothing and she didn't consider that a teenager could need anything more than the basics. There was no question of buying anything fashionable and she refused to buy anything at all which I wanted to choose for myself. It was tough to find jeans to fit me and my mother would say, in front of the salesperson that my body was disproportioned.

She told me that later, I would have trouble finding a husband because all my quality was in my head, not in my body. Although deep down, she was proud of my intelligence, she would rub it in that I did not have the makings of a good, marriageable *fräulein*. To her, a smart woman was not an attractive catch for most men. She often criticized me in this way, so that I would get red in the face because I believed it to be true. My teenage years were haunted by feelings of inadequacy which stemmed from this type of comment.

My father wanted me to watch the news and read the papers regularly and he looked askance at me if I did not. Although I was much too young at the time, I was made to believe that this was the right way to live. I tried to pay attention. I can remember watching the news and losing the context after only a few minutes. When I asked my father to give me some explanations, he told me to listen up and stop talking. It seemed he expected me to be born to it.

Sometimes the news would be in direct contradiction to something I had heard in school. I would get into big trouble with father when I questioned him about that. He told me to stop listening to the liars in the world outside. He would begin normally enough but then raise his voice and get angry at everybody for questioning the system all the time. His eyes would become like knives, at which point I would forget my question altogether, being afraid of his anger. He used to talk in the plural because he identified himself so completely with the party. It was no longer my father before me but a politician talking down to me. I would only find the truth on our national television, he would say, or in our newspapers, the books of Marx and Lenin or in his own words, period. That is why the story of our family is parallel to that of the system.

My political attitude seemed more important to my father than the fact that I was his daughter. It was what happened in the world outside which caused happiness or sadness in our family. In order to get love and respect I tried harder and harder to prove I had a positive attitude towards the society. I was hoping my father would see how much I was putting of myself into praising the socialist ideology. It never took him long to start singing the praises of the system himself. Then I would back up everything he said, wanting to show him how much I was on his side.

Other kids started to be very fed up of hearing the shiny phrases of the authorities and hardly cared about them any longer. I was still very convinced of the good intentions of the socialist state and I stored the questions of the kids who doubted, in my mind and went home to get answers. My idea was to get some ammunition with which to defend the system from its youthful detractors. I felt I had to be as strong as my parents expected me to be. The reason I allowed myself to ask questions of a spurious nature at home, was that I had immense confidence in the fact that my parents were my 'camerades'. This word implied a bond of trust and loyalty between a group of individuals, whether they were family or friends.

My father didn't believe that I was only bringing up these questions at home. Nor was he convinced of their origin. He suspected they were coming from my own heart. The confrontations continued and as I got older, because of my father's fear for my disloyalty, he actually came to believe it was true. The slogan '*Actions and words should be a unit*' was often used as an argument against people who asked questions or who put their fingers on the weak points of the society. They were criticized as naggers who talked too much without doing anything useful. At home, my father included me in that group. Yet at school, my teachers praised me for my unequivocal support of the system. This paradoxical situation became the rocky shore on which my personality later foundered.

Within the space of a half an hour, Father's supposed explanations to me would turn into a cascade of bitterness and hatred against anything and everything. If I dared to interrupt him to say that I understood now, he would say that I understood nothing. His line of reasoning now developed to the point where I would become the sole focus of his criticism. I had an unstable attitude, a basic mistrust of the system and anyway, a weak personality which would fall apart at the slightest pressure. I wished desperately for my mom to come home. She could turn his negative attention away from me. In the presence of my mother he was usually more cool and selected his words more carefully, even though he was still angry.

Again I was touching a very sensitive point of the society and therefore an equally delicate point for my father: asking the question why. He would get furious at that and I had no explanation for it. I was frightened, mixed up, anxious and wanted nothing more than to hide. He just wanted me to register and to accept what the system preached. That is where I failed. I could not agree to the assertion that the sun was shining when it was a cloudy day. I had become what he had shown me how to be: a stubborn defender of words.

One day in school, the class bully teased me once again, calling me a red cow. I could not hold myself back anymore and went after him. I tried to hit him, he tried to hit me. The others were making a circle around us, expecting a good show but a teacher came in and stopped the fight. I had reached my limits. I thought I was going to explode. What I had battled for so long to keep inside in order not to seem weak, was coming out of its own accord. Once again, I was put in the position of being disloyal both at home and at school and accused first on one side, then the other.

I was rarely happy with myself and anticipated school days with anxiety. Every morning at a quarter to six, I would dimly hear the banging doors of a coal-truck as it loaded up from a depot nearby. That noise was like a dull and tuneless peal of bells which bleakly heralded the new day. Although not yet quite awake, I would get anxious, thinking about the schoolday to come and waiting for the sound of my alarm clock. I got to know exactly when it would beep. There was a tiny mechanical noise that meant it was on the verge of going off. My hand would come down whack! on the clock before it could make a sound.

I would be instantly awake, breathing irregularly and within a few seconds, my mind would be flooded with thoughts of the coming day. I would start to move very fast, out of bed, into the bathroom, do twenty knee-bends, get dressed and then have breakfast. I forced myself to be disciplined. I had to, to get everything done because I didn't look forward to the coming morning and especially not going to school. Once out of the house I was back in the realm of the bullies, who I would always find on my way to school. I couldn't seem to find a way to protect myself.

When I told my parents about this sense of separation, they advised me to forget about the others. They were just jealous, they said and not worth worrying about. They frequently reminded me that others wanted to take advantage of me in order to find out more about my family. Their paranoid attitude taught me that silence is the real goal of a human being. I trusted their words yet after a while, I really started to miss the attention and respect of the other kids.

When I tried to discuss this with my parents again, their response was that I had nothing to complain about, that my life was so easy compared to theirs and that I should just be grateful. My father would imply that, had I been strong enough, I would not need the others. I was being put in a position of having to choose between my parents and my friends.

For my parents, it was out of the question to face the reality I expressed. They liked the world they were living in and were not ready to open their eyes to a different point of view. What I missed most in my childhood were gentle, loving explanations. Most of the wisdom they tried to teach me was transferred from a negative point of view. I was supposed to know many things by myself. I felt intimidated as they unloaded their 'truths of life' over my head, like buckets of cold water.

So the main lesson I learned from my parents was that life is a struggle and that it is selfish to live it other than in that light. From that I learned to feel guilty as soon as something felt easy. If things were fun I thought it couldn't be right and that something must be wrong with my attitude.

I felt incapable of meeting my parents' expectations and became defensive towards any criticism and aggressive towards all orders. I found it immensely difficult to keep on being a good socialist student and at the same time, was depressed at not being a cool teenager. I covered my insecurity with heated words and arguments and when I was close to crying in front of the class, my tongue would become as sharp as I could possibly make it. It wasn't a matter of choice. Caught between an endless crossfire, I was merely defending myself as best I could.

As I got more and more furious about my parents' refusal to listen, they finally came to the conclusion that I was a girl with a difficult character. That was the extent of their understanding. I tried to keep all these feelings locked inside but inevitably they turned into a hurricane of revolution.

Perhaps, this sort of thing was what led me to have

food-attacks after school. I would sometimes go to the bakery after school and buy a large quantity of buns which I would eat with butter and jam at one sitting. Or I would get some sweet cakes which I would eat on the street. Occasionally I would go home and empty whatever was in the breadbin in the kitchen. I would open the cupboard, get the bread out, butter a piece and eat it, butter the next and the next and the next until it was gone. I couldn't prepare it fast enough.

Once I had finished eating, I would wrap plastic bags around me and put on two jogging suits in order to sweat as much as possible. My idea was to somehow get rid of all the junk I had just put into myself. I would either run or ride a bike for half an hour or longer.

During the seventies, we would often see Russian soldiers marching in columns on the streets. They were going from their barracks down to the train station to leave the country. A girlfriend and I used to join them, walking beside the ranks. We used to skip beside them, holding our heads up and feeling heroic.

Sometimes they would hand us gifts such as buttons, medals or sugar bags with Russian lettering on them. Such presents were like treasures for me. The soldiers smelled of the garlic they ate so much and the tissue of their uniforms had a unique smell which I can never forget. I related the odor of these sturdy marchers and everything about them to thoughts of peace, friendship and safety. I imagine it was virtually the same sort of experience as my father had had as a hungry child, when he went reluctantly forward to the Russian soup kitchens at the end of the war.

My spoken Russian was not so good at that time. We

had only started to learn the language in the fifth grade. So we tried to communicate by speaking German with a Russian accent, hoping they would understand us. The nicest part of all was when they started to sing. I have always loved the sound of Russian choirs. They have beautiful melancholic voices which are full of powerful feelings. It would make my day when I heard those martial strains and I was proud as a peacock to have had their attention as I walked beside them.

Those happy occasions always warmed my heart and motivated me enough to be able to endure the constant pressure in school and at home. I wanted to support the system with all my heart. I felt that searching for truth was what would make the country and the people grow together. Problems were part of normal development, it seemed to me. Yet, the voice of the people could not be heard and I couldn't understand what the authorities were afraid of. They denied having any problems whatsoever and anyone who tried to put their finger on one was despised.

I was not aware of that as a teenager. I thought I was being so helpful by making my father aware of the opinions of others. It did not occur to me that he wasn't even interested in hearing what people had to say. In his strategy and that of the system, the only thing which counted was the facade of success which was erected and maintained in every quarter of that ideal society. Based on my experiences, I began to believe myself that 'problems' *per se*, were bad, considering the kind of trouble they seemed to cause.

Frankfurt (Oder), 1980

At about the age of thirteen, I started to get interested in my father's guitar. I used to take it out and try to make sense of the strings. I had no idea how it was supposed to work. My father showed me how to play the chords A, D and E. I was incredibly happy. Right away I fell in love with it. Soon I was practicing my first song. There was something about the fact that I could create this sound that was fascinating to me. It was as if I had found a friend or a new companion. Little did I know just how important a discovery it was.

I also love to sing. Because of the restrictions, I was not able to hear much of the music coming from the West and especially not music for young people. Only western songs which were carefully selected by the government were ever played on our radio. In the house, I found LP's of Milva, Nana Mouskouri and Mireille Mathieu. These were some of the first artists I sang along with. I wrote down the lyrics so I could learn them more easily. When I came home from school, I often spent an hour singing along with the LP's and eating my favorite meal of white bread and strawberry jam.

Only after that would I start to do my homework. Then I played guitar or read my fairy tale books. I was a member of a library and sometimes I consumed two books a day. I would get a rush to read them. It was like a drug that filled me with energy. My reading habits were a bit like my eating habits. I would feel an insatiable urge to consume one or the other. Sometimes I would read until I was dizzy.

Fairy tales influenced me greatly. They taught me that people have to go through tough times but that the good-hearted always prevail in the end. I am grateful to have had this source of happiness around because it's what kept my dreams alive. Books and music were my true friends. Nobody could keep me from reading or singing.

Criticism from my parents was always just around the corner. My parents were afraid that I was gluing my mind with dreams. I knew that I was freeing my mind through those same dreams. In this desert of monotonous development, it was easy to be trapped in the pattern of a robot-like production. On the outside, I already acted like one. There was a lot of talk about individual development, yet the system did not follow its own principles. It got caught up in trying to make all lives equal and in so doing, it had to insist that everybody thought the same way.

When I requested membership in the Communist party at the age of eighteen, I was refused. At first I couldn't believe it but as I looked back over the previous year, I began to understand some things about our society which I hadn't noticed before. We had been asked to join the Party at the age of seventeen. At that time there had been a wave of independent thinking and many people had simply refused the offer. For my part, I had decided to wait. I replied that I wanted to take the time to think over such a serious decision. It was a big commitment to make and I felt I was not then ready for it.

I could scarcely credit that that decision would have such far-reaching consequences. The refusal that I received shook my belief completely. I now began to understand just how the system worked. If you gave the slightest sign of not being completely pliable, you were labeled and put into a category which included the most undesirable intellectual elements in the society. It was just not acceptable to ask questions or to have a mind of your own. At this stage of its development, East German socialism was like a religion which demanded complete obedience to its precepts.

I still couldn't understand why I was being classed with the others. The 'others' were the so-called unreliable elements in society. There I stood, having spent my teenage years fighting the good fight, having lost friends because I was *too* convinced about my society. Now I was being rejected by the very system that I had sacrificed my early youth for. The system had meant everything to me, that's why I tried so hard to match up to the slogans. I had taken it all so seriously. It turned out that the society wasn't half as serious as I was. That was a hard lesson. I learned not to base my life on something I couldn't control.

Soviet Union, 1980

When I was not quite fourteen years old, I got to live out one of my biggest dreams. One day in class it was announced that five of us would be eligible for a trip to the Soviet Union. It was a sort of prize, offered by the GDR government as a reward for diligent pupils. While I was flaming to go on such a journey, some of the other kids showed little or no interest. It was left up to the class, with the teacher's guidance, to decide who should be in the group. The main criteria were effort and marks in school. Fortunately that favored me greatly and I was one of the lucky ones chosen to go.

We left in winter time. My parents were happy for me to be able to undertake a special trip like that. My mother and I went out to buy a nice winter coat with which to confront the cold of Moscow. The day of departure arrived and we went to join a gang of kids from other schools who were also going on the trip with us. There were about fifty of us altogether. As we waited at the station, we chattered eagerly about the fun we would have going to sleep on a train as it rolled along all night.

I could see this was to be a very special experience for me, even before we left. It was a long time since I had been exclusively with other young people who were from a similar background to me. The kids all seemed to care for one another immediately and it was no wonder. We were all the best pupils from our different schools and we had much in common. I felt a real sympathy amongst the group and couldn't sense a trace of hostility. That relieved me a lot. I also brought my guitar with me, thinking we might all sing along together.

The train travelled via Poland in order to get to the Soviet Union. Finally we reached the border and began to pass through the Russian countryside. I was struck by the sight of blue and green roofs on the houses. The villages were very pleasing to look at, in contrast with our own. I spent long periods gazing out at the passing scene, ever so happy to be in that land.

For two days and a night we travelled along. We were served tea from a typical Russian samovar whenever we wanted it. I couldn't believe I was finally in the land of my dreams. I had a deep sympathy for this country and its people. To me it was a symbol of peace and friendship. This was partly due to my education but also because of my favorite fairy tales, which came from Russia. Their folklore is wonderful and their fairy tales are rich in love and wisdom.

First we went to Moscow where we visited Red Square. The Kremlin towers were so beautiful. What impressed me more, however, was our visit to see the corpse of Lenin. It was guarded like a treasure inside a mausoleum. The line-up outside was incredible. It moved so slowly. It took us about an hour before we got to see the famous Soviet founder. Nobody was allowed to talk inside so we slipped piously through the room, meter by meter.

The soldiers kept guard over the corpse in all honor. I looked at Lenin's face which seemed like wax. I was surprised to see how physically small he was and I wondered had he shrunk while he was lying there all those years.

Our second city was St Petersburg and there we had the chance to visit the 'Aurora'. It was the ship which had fired the cannon shot to begin the October Revolution in 1917 and was justly famous. Altogether we spent about a week in the Soviet Union. On our way back we had a great time. The road home seemed less long to us because we knew each other by then and everyone was in a good mood. We talked and laughed all the way.

Eventually, I felt it was time to take out my guitar. I knew some popular songs that everyone could sing along with. Singing and laughing we arrived back in our hometown. Most of us would have liked to continue with this celebration of life but our parents were waiting at the station for us. Before long, the happy retinue had disappeared in a variety of buses and cars, on their way back to normal life.

Frankfurt (Oder), 1981

A girl from my class brought a newspaper article to school. The city choir was looking for younger members. We both got excited about it and wanted to give it a try. We were accepted after passing a test. I couldn't believe it! Another dimension was suddenly added to my life. I enjoyed the work in the choir right from the start. After a couple of practices, my friend dropped out but not me. I continued.

The choir had six different voice ranges. Each section had to learn their part separately from the others. It took patience to master the complicated voices and it was often dry work. Sometimes we would monotonously repeat the same line until the whole song was learned. Only then did the choir come together and try it out. That was the fun part, when we were able to earn the first fruits of our long practices.

The blending of our voices in such beautiful harmonies was tremendously satisfying. Weak at first but then becoming richer in sound, the range would develop until the building resounded with the combined strength of the choir. It would move me so much, the tears would run down my cheeks. I even became a little frustrated because my tears sometimes kept me from singing. I remembered the power of Russian choirs I had heard in the past and was proud to have a chance of singing in a choir myself.

When I first joined the choir, the person singing beside me could barely hear me. My voice wasn't trained, so I couldn't sing very loudly. She advised me to practice while I passed the vacuum-cleaner. That way I wouldn't disturb anybody and at the same time, I could get used to overcoming a strong sound with my voice. Besides doing that, I took weekly lessons in voice training, which were included in the membership of the choir. When I practiced at home, I would get mad when my throat started hurting or when there was a scratchy sound in my voice. So I went to the lessons with even greater enthusiasm, curious to learn some technical tricks.

I was very consistent in the pursuit of my new hobby and my voice got stronger with time. Once in a while we had a so-called choir-weekend. We took a bus and spent the weekend practicing some place else. It also provided a chance for me to develop my guitar playing. The young kids spent much of their time showing each other musical tricks. Everybody seemed to know something, so we were all able to share in this musical experience. It was a time of expansion for us and I enjoyed it immensely.

In 1981, I had to make up my mind about my future profession. I was interested in working in a daycare. I remembered my own kindergarten-teacher playing the guitar and singing songs with us. My parents told me that if I was interested in working with children, I could also become a school-teacher. I didn't like the idea very much but my parents tried to talk me into it. They said it would mean higher qualifications, better pay and greater recognition from the society. They valued all of these things highly and so they set about trying to make it happen.

They invited my teacher home and talked to him about my future as a teacher. They all agreed that it would be the ideal profession for me. They then turned their attention towards convincing me that it was the best thing to do. Yet I was only fourteen years old. How could I be sure what it was I wanted to work at for the rest of my life?

In our society, it was thought that a profession, once learned, would remain our field forever. It would be hard if not impossible to change direction or to learn another profession. We had to write a letter to the college we wanted to attend, soliciting a position in our chosen field. In most professions, letters of solicitation had to be sent at the age of sixteen. Because of the long-term planning necessary for the teaching profession, I had to come up with an answer at age fourteen.

My parents tried to encourage me by saying that I would be the first person in our family history to go to college. Besides, it fit perfectly into the picture they imagined for themselves. They were parents working for the Secret Service and their daughter would be responsible for educating the new socialist youth. It was politically very acceptable. To have been a mere hairdresser or something would not have been'good enough' in that context.

So I was warned not to throw the opportunity away.

My decision-making process having been so completely manipulated, I began to feel guilty about not becoming a teacher. I believed that to reject the profession would be the equivalent of showing an unwillingness to support the system. I told my parents that I was interested in working for the Secret Service but they said it wouldn't be possible. My father commented that they needed quite different people from me in that line of work. The way he brought it out made it sound as though I was not good enough for the job. In fact, both my parents but particularly my mother, were afraid to encourage me to join Security. They intimated that I would be better off without that kind of pressure.

I began to worry that, if I became a teacher, I might not have a chance to sing and play the guitar. I wanted this to be more than just a hobby. These concerns were eventually waived by the suggestion that I might be able to teach music. Finally I wrote out the letter, asking to be considered for an eventual position at the appropriate college.

Part of this early solicitation process, was to explain the reasons for choosing our profession. Mine added up to the following: I love children, I want to be part of their development towards becoming individual, socialist personalities and that would be my contribution to strengthening our socialist country.

About one year later I received my acceptance at the Institute for Teacher Development. I was invited to an interview where I was asked if I could give any other reasons for my choice of occupation. There was really nothing else that I could think of to explain why I wanted to be a teacher. The truth was that I was not very motivated. I almost had to say that this whole teacher thing was my parents' idea, but I didn't.

Meanwhile, high school moved into its last year. I was sixteen and more in love with music than ever before. I was invited to sing with another group of young people. It was more of a choral society which performed mainly classical pieces. I was now out of the house in the early evening four times a week, practicing in the choir. We performed at several social occasions and we gave concerts at Christmas. My parents visited one of them and were very proud of me. My activity was socially very appreciated. In the school reports at the end of the year, I was praised for spending my free time so sensibly.

The conflict started to arise when I told my parents about my wish to study music. I was a bit older then and beginning to speak up for what I wanted to do in life, for what I felt like spending my energy on. This seemed to be a nightmare for my parents. They felt that their perfect plan was in danger of falling apart. Everything was well-organized and now it appeared I wanted to make trouble and ruin the plans they had for me. Their reaction was the following:

"This can't be true, she is throwing her chance away. You can't spend your life singing. Work is what's important and it's the only healthy thing to do. You have to prove yourself to us. Show us that you are capable of something. Something more sensible than singing. You can't do in life what you want. You have to accept your responsibilities. Our socialist-communist matter is the most important thing. Without it the world will not develop and change for the better. If you exclude yourself from that you are not worth much. You don't have the guts to look life in the face. You are lazy and want others to work. You only know how to nag instead of making things better through your work."

It was not only what they said, it was also the way it was shouted at me. I would have loved to have a normal conversation with my parents. I missed talking with them. They were always talking *at* me. When I would say to my father:

"I would like to say something to you," he would reply:

"You have nothing to say to me, you are only allowed to ask me something."

In those years, my teenage years, my father worked night shifts. On returning home from school, my one thought was not to disturb him. I knew only too well what the afternoon would bring anyway so I hoped he wouldn't wake up too soon. I love my dad. I tried to do things right, to get his approval, to please him. But he just drove me straight back up the wall each time he put me down with his unkind words.

On the weekends, sitting together at the breakfast table, we would listen to the radio while eating. As soon as the news came on, my father would begin to comment on it and expected us to participate in a discussion. My mother would automatically contribute some thought or other but I found it hard to concentrate so early in the day. I was often dizzy in the mornings and the weekends were my special time when I didn't have to be in school at seven o'clock. My father found it difficult to accept any reluctance on my part, for whatever reason so he would take me to task for being lazy and disinterested, once again.

Although I was used to his impulsive nature, I was getting fed up with it. His angry eyes could spread so much hate that I was afraid of being hit, but my revolt against his authority was even stronger. I talked back and called him an 'asshole'. I ran into my room and locked the door. He banged against it, yelling that I should open it or he would knock it down. I told him that I didn't want to be hit. He yelled:

"Open the door!" I replied:

"Only if you stop being so angry." My father had only ever hit me once but I felt he was so furious that he seemed out of control. I felt threatened by his anger which was thick in the air around me. Yet to be trapped in that room, hearing my father getting ever more angry, was worse. I finally turned the key and ran to hide in the corner. Nothing happened but the vibes in the air and the sound of his voice had already nearly scared the life out of me. My heart was having convulsions and I was feeling terrible. I was not enjoying being with my father at all. I had so much anger against him now. I was fed up of living like a mouse.

On another occasion when my father got angry like that, I went running out of the house. I was too terrified to stay. I didn't worry that I had no shoes on. I just had to get away from that mess. I stopped after a few hundred meters and hid in a house entranceway, out of breath and shaking. Half an hour later I slunk home, not knowing what to expect. I had nowhere else to go and the uncertainty about what might happen next made me enter the apartment with a feeling of despair.

Again I wished I could become invisible.

Yet there was no storm awaiting me. My parents went about their routine, almost ignoring the fact that I had returned to my room. For the next half hour I was on the alert for another attack, prepared to defend myself. Nothing happened. Slowly we began some family talk and it was as if nothing had ever occurred. I felt more than a little mistrust towards the sudden peace and wondered why neither of my parents tried to talk to resolve the situation. Their method seemed to be to keep quiet about it and to go on with life, ignoring the past.

For my part, I was happy to be able to breathe comfortably again and did not really want to bring it up either. This was how it had always been at our place so I grew up thinking it to be the normal aftermath to crises and confrontations. By the time I was reaching my adult years, there was a lot of stuff hanging around in the air.

It didn't occur to me that my father was sad and frustrated. I didn't know that he had chosen to work for the government, instead of pursuing a musical career. I remember him telling me about having taken saxophone and clarinet lessons. To attend them, he had to get to the nearby city, about five kilometers from his village. He decided to go back and forth by jogging the whole distance. He must have been in great physical shape to have been able to do that. It also shows him as a strong, willing and motivated young man who had a goal he wanted to achieve. Yet, in spite of that, he came to believe or was made to believe, that the music he loved so much could only be a hobby.

Whatever his motives were, they were certainly

enshrouded in the belief that this was the only right thing to do. He felt that to have followed his musical inclinations would have been selfish. Even though my father was proud of me in some ways because I showed some musical ability, he seemed to hate it at the same time. He probably expected the same sacrifice of me that he had agreed to. Or maybe he was frustrated about his own decision. Maybe he was jealous, seeing me doing what he had wanted to do. He always insisted so much on putting aside personal interests. Maybe he needed this anger in order to convince himself that he was doing the right thing. It was like a sort of strange counter-balance for the fact that he had given something, so important, up.

The interference of my parents' work in our private lives also meant that I was obliged to give them information about people I met. I was not supposed to have contacts they didn't know about since they needed to check them all out for security reasons. As I was longing for the approval of my parents, I never kept anything from them. They would ask me things like:

"Who is that? What's their background? What do their parents' do?" If they learned that I had already given our phone number or address or even just my family name, they would fall on me as though I was to blame in some way for trying to deceive them. By being honest I had hoped to earn their respect. Yet, the only thing I ever seemed to achieve was to be denied permission to see these people again. Noone seemed to be worthy of their trust nor was anyone ever an appropriate companion for me.

Besides that, my parents always wanted to know exactly where I was going and with whom. Even if it was the most harmless thing, like the choir, they warned me to be solidly on my guard against bad influences. My father expressed his especial doubts about my ability to resist manipulation. That was no doubt because he knew very well, how easily and completely he could manipulate me himself. Their caution was like a chain around me. I wasn't encouraged to hang out with kids of my own age after school. I might have learned bad things like smoking or talking against socialism. Perhaps I might also have lost the drive to be a good student.

One day I went to buy a pack of cigarettes but I couldn't live with myself. I felt so bad, thinking I was betraying my parents. I went to my father and showed him the cigarettes, crying that I was sorry for being bad. I hoped coming forward by myself would be appreciated. Unfortunately it didn't change anything in father's aggressive approach. As usual, he talked down to me:

"You see, I told you it doesn't do any good for you to hang out with the others. They have nothing in their heads but nonsense." My parents gave me to understand that the outside world was a threat to my development. As they were fond of repeating, I had all I needed at home and at school. Not knowing how to avoid it, I allowed my parents to have full control over me. I didn't know how to change that anyway. I began to mistrust other people because I believed they were the ones who caused me the trouble at home. I thought my parents were the only ones on my side and I could not imagine going on without them. At the same time, I felt terrible to be such a brat at home. I blamed myself, because I didn't seem to be able to love anyone at all. At that time, it seemed as though I hated life.

It is a fact that my parents were as tough on themselves as they were on others, with regards to having contacts with western people. On one of our summer vacations at my grandparents', an incident took place which shows just how keen they were on being consistent in the political context.

On those vacations, my sister and I sometimes went to play with some cousins of ours who lived in a nearby village. It was about five kilometers from my grandparents' place. Usually, my parents would drive us over there before lunch and then come and get us in the afternoon. We loved going there, it was always good fun.

On one of those occasions, when we were playing together by the side of the road, our parents' car suddenly appeared beside us. They both hurried out of the car, which was all packed up and instructed us to leave what we were doing and come with them at once. Jana and I were caught by surprise and wanted to know what the rush was for. Only after we were on the move did we realize that we were on our way home to Frankfurt (Oder).

In disbelief, I asked for an explanation. We had hardly had time to say goodbye to our cousins and had left them where they stood, comprehending nothing. As we went further on our way, we realized that we had not said goodbye to our grandparents, either. We felt extremely sad about the abrupt ending to these holidays.

My mother tried to explain the reason for our sudden return. It happened that, while the two of us were over playing with our cousins, some of the family's relatives from the West had arrived without warning, at our grandparents'. Since my parents' positions within the government did not permit them to have any Western contacts whatsoever, they were obliged to leave the house at once.

This was a delicate situation for everyone concerned. All our relatives were perfectly aware that such a rule existed and that it applied to us. The aunt who lived in the neighboring village had close family ties with the West and our holidays were always organized in such a way that we would never come across them. Having them turn up unannounced placed my parents in a very compromising situation and they somehow felt as though there was deliberate disrespect involved. Everybody knew perfectly well the problems it could cause them with their organization. I can't help thinking, in retrospect, that the whole scenario might have been purposefully mounted by our relatives. Maybe they just wanted to demonstrate their displeasure with my father's one and only subject of conversation: politics.

In fact, it was already a borderline case for them to be seeing my uncle and aunt. It would have been possible for them to have been denied the right to visit them for exactly the reason for which we were leaving in such a hurry. They were too close to these Westerners, a fact which was of course known to the State Security. So my parents felt that there was only one thing to do and, looking back, I can understand their decision. That was the sort of bizarre impact that my parents' professional lives could have on our private lives. As children, we didn't know how to deal with it. In a subtle way, it made us build a stronger barrier between us and the 'others'.

My sister, because she was younger, was able to be an observer of what was going on at home. By the time she was a teenager I had moved out to go to college. When I came home for a visit, it was a shock for me to see the kingdom that she had built for herself. Her room, which in the past had been our room, was papered with Madonna posters. She was popular in school, she knew how to socialize. She had a cassette player and listened to western music. She was allowed to have friends over. She had a good sense of humour and hung out with the people she liked. She dressed as she liked and on top of all that, she smoked.

In reality, it was just the life of an average teenager, but it seemed like a magic kingdom to me. She also got along better with my parents than I ever had. Oh, she would get into trouble with them at times but she had the knack of not letting it get to her. She told me that she never wanted to get hurt as I had. So she went ahead doing her things, leaving my parents speechless.

Yet, the power struggle of my parents did affect her too. One time she came home and her room was being renovated. All her posters were gone and she was surrounded by white walls. So she knows about invasion of privacy. In my parents' opinion, any kind of problem was the fault of my sister and myself. They only accepted the responsibility for success.

To live so far away is an incredible relief for me. They can't understand how I can cope without them, so alone and far away. If they only knew. My mother admits that they were less tough on my sister. They did not see everything as being so serious anymore. As the first-born, I got to taste most of their anxiety.

Neuzelle, 1984

When it was time to move into college in Neuzelle, I was desperate. I did not want to be away from home. I had been taught that the world was a scary place and I was afraid of it. It did not cross my mind that the over-protectiveness of my parents might have something to do with my inability to mix with people, or that their control over every aspect of my life might have been the cause of my anger and lack of self confidence. I could only guess that something was wrong when I compared myself to others, yet I didn't know what it was. I was brought up to believe that things were either black or white. That was the central conflict in my life. I was constantly fighting a battle with my own intuition because it was often telling me that what I was hearing from my parents was not quite right.

On the conscious level, I so wanted to believe everything I was told that I got used to deceiving myself. It was like a strange sort of addiction, against which there was no apparent defense. I couldn't have imagined leaving home, nor could I think of life without my parents. And yet, though I couldn't understand it at the time, their power over me was slowly destroying my spirit.

The day of my departure for college came. My parents drove me to Neuzelle which is about forty five minutes from Frankfurt (Oder). I had never spoken to them about my fears of leaving home. At the time I thought it must have been just normal anxiety about the unknown. When we arrived at the college we found ourselves facing some huge old brick buildings with a stone wall going all around them. It was explained to us that this was a former seminary for nuns and monks. It looked like a place where people had been confined. Behind the gate I could see the church and I was somehow scared by the serious expression of this place. I was so depressed and imagined that that was how it must feel to be put in prison.

When I saw all the students gathering in the middle of these buildings, I got even more scared. Now I had to face the next challenge of having to integrate myself. All of us were wearing those blue shirts of the Youth Organization and the students looked curiously at everybody who entered the gate. My parents said that it was time to go and I looked over to the others with a great deal of insecurity. Turning back to my parents I could see that they did not seem very happy themselves. For a moment I hoped that they would say:

"Come Pina, let's go back home. We are not going to leave you behind in this old and dirty looking place." I thought that my being so close to a church might get them worried about me falling under its 'bad' influence, so that they would change their mind. They didn't but nevertheless tried to comfort me by saying that I was going to be home every weekend.

When I realized that there was no way out, I tried a last vague protest:

"I don't want to stay here." It was actually more like a question as to whether I really needed to stay there. I guess if I had been about to start studying music in the same place I would have been far less pessimistic towards those dark surroundings. When my parents kissed me goodbye, I felt as one newly abandoned. In my heart I knew, right there at the beginning, that I didn't at all want to become a teacher.

Now I had no choice but to simply fight my tears and swallow my sadness. When my parents drove off in their car, my first impulse was to run away. Yet I stayed because I had been taught to be strong in doing things that did not fulfill my personal desires. I walked towards the others and got anxious when I saw some of them put their heads together as I approached. Trying to put all my worries aside, I went to find the group of students I belonged to.

After the classes were organized I found myself sitting in a room with twenty other girls and a teacher. Even though on one level, I was much annoyed about being there, I was somewhat curious about the things to come. I hesitated to show any obvious interest and as I looked around, I could see that the other students were also a bit shy. As the teacher started to talk about the functioning of the school, some began to ask questions. Later, when it was my turn to talk a little about myself and my motives for becoming a teacher, I made sure that the tone of my voice expressed the boredom I felt about being there. Looking at the teacher, I tried my best to put a rebellious expression on my face. This kind of attitude was so untypical of me when compared to the efforts I had always made to be a good student. I had decided to no longer play that role and hoped that I would somehow be dismissed from this college for bad marks and lack of motivation.

At the end of this first encounter, our teacher handed each of us a paper which we were ordered to sign. When I saw what was written on it I got very upset. It said that by signing this paper we obliged ourselves to study for the best marks possible, in the interest of our society and to work at least three years in that profession after having finished the four years of college. I stared at the paper and felt like ripping it up. Then I looked at the others to see what their reaction was. Some had already signed and others were talking. I turned to the girl sitting beside me and asked her what she thought about that. She said that it was normal since we studied for free at the expense of the society and this obligation was our offer to the society in return. I had to agree to that but said to myself that they should have filled my place with someone who really wanted to become a teacher.

There was something else that motivated me to behave in such a rebellious fashion. My experience in school had shown me that lazy kids were better integrated in the class and that diligent pupils were often picked on for their efforts. I was tempted to try a different approach here and to belong to those 'cool and lazy' students. I did not take into consideration that most students came here with a lot of determination and motivation about becoming a teacher. So I was actually preparing myself for a position that would make approval from others difficult once again.

Not being aware of that then, I still hesitated to sign. I

began to get more angry because I felt trapped. I said to the teacher that noone could oblige me to sign such a thing. Everybody seemed surprised at my attitude and the teacher tried to convince me to do the right thing. By that time I was surprised at myself, since I had never before dreamed of rebelling in school. I got a little scared because it felt so weird not to automatically do what I was told. I signed.

The next day my father was called to the college and had a talk with my teacher. I was also present and when the teacher asked questions my father answered for me. He said that I was going to be a good student and that I would put all my efforts into becoming a fine teacher for our society. I could clearly feel his embarrassment about being there and said that I never wanted to become a teacher. This was more or less ignored by both of them and the teacher, who did not know much about me, came to the conclusion that I was one of those students who didn't care much about life or what they were doing.

The year went on and I could hardly deal with the exterior image that I had built of myself. I knew my true strengths and was mad about making others think that I was stupid. Yet, I had made a friend who also played guitar and it was with her that I hung out all the time. She was five years older than most of the students and was certain of her decision to become a teacher. Her mother was a teacher as well. That reminded me that my own mother had often talked about her wish of being a teacher. I asked myself whether I was on this earth to live other people's lives or not. It was a reflection of our society and my parents stood in front of a door, blocking my entry to where I wanted to go. Instead, they were going to lock me up in a space that they decided would be mine.

Lake Helene, Summer 1985

In the summer of 1985 I had my first boyfriend whom I met through his sister. She was my best friend at college. In August, I went with both of them for a few days camping with friends. I wish I could recall other more pleasant memories from what should have been an enjoyable weekend together.

Instead, I can see myself stumbling over tent-ropes, having completely lost my orientation. In my mind I was vaguely asking myself the questions: where do I come from and where am I going? I was staggering and in my hand I carried a precious bottle of cognac. Sadness was digging into me and I was becoming more and more agitated. I was fed up of repressing it all. I didn't want to swallow anymore. I had been force-fed for too long. I wanted to turn it on to the outside and the alcohol took care of that nicely.

In that state of mind, nobody could stop me from showing exactly how I felt. It made me want to sing and dance and cry, all at the same time. It felt good to be picked up by my boyfriend who then carried me I don't know where. Nor did I care. It was just nice to be taken care of. It was good not to have to walk. I had very satisfactorily lost all sense of direction.

I asked myself how had I got there in the first place? Then I remembered that I had been alone in my parents' apartment. They had gone on vacation with my sister and I had stayed behind to finish some work for college. It was the summer holidays and I had gotten through my freshman year, making sure to finish with the worst possible marks so that everyone would know that I could never become a teacher.

Just a few days before, I had come back from a trip to Czechoslovakia with a group of students. It had been a pleasant experience. I especially adored the natural beauty of the mountains. Yet there was something that kept me from experiencing a deeper enjoyment. For some weeks, sadness had been building up inside, manifesting its presence more clearly every day and gradually taking over any positive feelings which remained.

Sitting alone in the apartment, I was bored to death and did not even want to look at the papers which I had to work on for college. Nothing could make me touch the stuff. I could not make sense out of anything regarding the direction of my life. When I thought about the next day, the next week, the end of the holidays, the beginning of the second year in college, I was fearful. I didn't know where to turn or how to escape from something that I could not even clearly identify. All I knew was that darkness was surrounding me despite the beautiful sunshine.

I began to search for a way to stop this feeling so I looked around for some alcohol and found the cognac.

It was my first encounter with that substance and I was surprised at the way it made me feel.

It was exactly the effect I had been looking for: to paralyze my brain and give space to my choking emotions. Now I felt strong enough to face the world. Feeling wonderfully dizzy, I grabbed a few things and was soon on my way to see my friends. They lived in another city, so I hitchhiked my way over to them. On the road, a Russian army truck picked me up and I was amazed to discover how well I could communicate in Russian. I had been learning the language for five years and it was the first time I had had a chance to use it. I felt as light as a feather but when I arrived at my friends' place, they put me straight to bed. I had no problems whatsoever falling asleep. I felt safe and well taken care of. When I woke, up they invited me to join them for a couple of days camping. I welcomed the chance not to be alone. It gave me a feeling of belonging somewhere and I was glad to be facing a different reality from the one at home.

Yet being there on the camp-site didn't change any of my mixed up emotions. I still felt lonely and nobody could replace the empty space I had inside. The only thing which made sense was to keep on flooding my insides with alcohol. I am not sure how my friends explained this behavior of mine but we didn't talk about it. Probably I was far too drunk to have a decent conversation. After two days, I hitchhiked back home again.

Once home, I started to feel guilty about the way I'd behaved. I considered myself as a failure, as a freak of nature and could not figure out what to do about it. Life seemed to be nothing but a black hole. I tried to pull myself out of it by putting all my college papers on the table in the living room. I sat and stared at them for a long time. I could not understand what was keeping me from getting on with my work. Imperceptibly at first, my emotions started to rise and I realized that my heart had begun to beat wildly. I began to feel as if I was in a hurricane, not knowing which tree to hold on to. I got up and turned on the radio. I switched the channels until I found an American one, which was being broadcasted from a U.S. military base in the West. I put the volume up high and went back to sit at the table. I felt deeply rebellious and enjoyed the freedom of listening to something which was normally forbidden. I didn't care about not being able to understand a word of what was said.

Suddenly the solution flashed into my mind. There was a way to get away from all this. I did have a power that noone else had. I had control over my own life. The memory came back to me of the year before, when I had taken my teddy bear and a knife and gone to sit alone on a little hill by the road. With a wooden stick, I slowly wrote those words in the sand: *'Bury me in Berlin'*. Then I looked up at the sky, dreaming of happiness. Slowly I moved the knife to my artery but I didn't really want to hurt myself. I got up and ran back home.

This time I was going to do it. I began to think about how it would be done. Since the idea had come to me, I felt at peace with myself. It was odd for me to realize how good I felt to be able to see a way out. I had a choice after all. It was as if a heavy curtain had fallen from in front of my eyes and at the same time I felt a gentle sorrow that my recourse had to be so desperate. I felt incapable of dealing with the veil of sadness which surrounded me as soon I thought of the reality of my life.

I planned on taking an overdose of sleeping pills. I decided to buy them next morning at the pharmacy. After having made this plan, I put the papers away and went to sleep. When I woke up in the morning, I was as determined as ever. I got dressed and went to buy the pills. Each pack contained ten of them and when I asked for two packs the salesperson told me that they only sold one pack at a time. I bought one pack and went back home. I rang at the door of my neighbor and spoke to the boy of fourteen who was alone at home. I asked him to get me a second pack of sleeping pills and a half an hour later, he handed them to me.

Then I was alone, standing in the kitchen with twenty pills and a bottle of schnapps. I tried to listen to my inside to see whether or not my sadness was still telling me that I was doing the right thing. Then I started to rinse each pill down my throat with a sip of alcohol. Since I did not want my parents to find me in the apartment I left the house and began to walk away fast. As I reached the highway not far off, I began to stumble. I got more and more dizzy and tears started rolling over my face. I kept on going and called Mama, Mama. I cried out for help, believing that it was too late for any. Noisy cars passed at high speed and drowned out the sound of my voice. Dragging my body along the side of the road I looked at the clouds above me. Trying to take one more step, I lost sight of the ground under my feet, fell down and fainted.

I remember the strangest sensation. Somebody was trying to choke me. I couldn't breathe. I wanted to cry out to them to let go of me or I would suffocate! I could see and hear nothing. I could only think and feel that I was being killed. My fear grew and in the greatest despair I hit out around me. Just when I thought I was dying, the pressure stopped.

I could hardly open my eyes but I could make out the shape of a man standing over me. He seemed to be talking but I could not understand. He persisted and I began to understand a little but could neither move nor talk on my own account. I fell asleep. When I woke up I had no notion of time nor any idea where I was. My head was spinning as I tried to recognize something around me. There was a man who I thought I might have seen before. He approached me, saying he was a doctor. I was so mixed up and told him that somebody had tried to kill me. He replied that it was I who had tried to do that and explained that he had pumped out my stomach to remove the bad things I had put in there.

Only then did I remember what had happened and it was a strange feeling to be alive and lying in that bed. I was vaguely disappointed that my life and its struggle was going to start all over again. He asked me if I was feeling better and I said no. He asked me if I really wanted to die and I said yes. He asked me why and I said I didn't know. I turned my head to the window and saw that it was dark outside. I just wanted to be alone and not to talk with anybody. I doubted if anybody could or was really willing to understand me. After my experience, all that counted in this world was to go through life without caring about feelings. I did not want to be a part of that kind of life.

Shortly after that I fell asleep again and woke up the next day, sometime in the afternoon. I was told that my parents were on their way to the hospital. I had no idea of what to say to them or how to face them. I had turned my back on both myself and my family and did not know how to face the consequences of my action, which I knew would probably be interpreted as a betrayal. At three o'clock in the afternoon they arrived and I was standing outside the hospital to receive them. They came towards me in a very stiff way. As they approached, I could see their concerned faces. I welcomed them with a shy smile. We had a hard time looking at each other and they didn't know what to say any more than I did. My father asked me why and I could not really express why. My mother said:

"You give us nothing but trouble. You have no reason to do something like that." I am not sure if they were really ever interested in any deep explanation I might have had. They seemed to have space only for the pain and embarrassment I had caused them. They went inside to have a talk with the psychologist. It didn't take very long and then it was my turn to go into his office while my parents waited outside.

The psychologist asked me about my motives and I explained to him that I saw no sense in living anymore. Seeking for a concrete reason, he asked me if it had anything to do with my boyfriend. I didn't seem to be able to convince him that he had had nothing to do with it. I suppose my explanation lacked any other clear motives and he wanted to fix on something. I had a hard time myself to put into words what was going on inside of me but I knew that the matter was much more complex than just a boyfriend. Besides, nothing had happened in our relationship that could have caused me to make that kind of decision. He was actually one of the rare people who were open to my thoughts and feelings.

The psychologist finished the conversation at this point and we went outside to my parents. He suggested counseling and I heard my father say:

"We are handling this by ourselves, there is no need for outside support. Pina has just to learn to accept life and to listen better to what we say." We drove home and from then on this subject was covered with silence and whenever it was touched upon, it was put back in a secret drawer very fast. It was treated as something to be ashamed of, to be hidden and forgotten. It was a hurtful memory that did not belong in their lives because there was no reason for it to have happened. They came to regard it more as an accident that would not be repeated because they were going to protect me even more strongly against bad influences from then on.

I remember asking myself:

"Is this all the compassion they have after such a desperate act?" I had not expected to survive the attempt and knowing with what determination I had carried it out, I was shocked to see how little it made my parents react, at least on the outside. Was this how little I mattered to them? I thought they might have asked if I needed any help. They might have enquired into the reasons for my doing what I had done. Yet, instead of asking me how *I* felt, they talked about how I had hurt them. I realized that their lack of interest was one of the main reasons for my action in the first place.

After this experience it was out of the question for me to repeat myself and I was determined to go and get my share of life. I gave up the illusion that I was going to be taken care of and from then on, I decided to carry the flag of faith in my own hands.

The holidays were soon finished and I had to go back to college. Except for my boyfriend and his sister, who was in the same class with me, nobody was told about the situation. Life went on and in the following months, I still had problems getting back on track. I still exposed my boyfriend to emotional dramas. My parents were still holding him and his influence on me responsible for what had happened. In December, he finally split from me, unable to accept a responsibility that wasn't his. To have lost him was a message to me that I had to shape up if I wanted love to be a part of my life.

I didn't talk much about myself and did so even less after the incident during summer. In one of the reports that we all receive at the end of each year, it said that I should use the help of the collective to solve certain personal problems I was having. Actually I had closed myself up on purpose. My experiences of talking openly about how I felt had been too negative.

Now I was about to turn eighteen. My parents used this occasion to tell me what they thought I hadn't heard often enough.

Frankfurt (Oder), December 1985

Dear Pina – our dear daughter!

Your 18th birthday is for us, for our family, a special occasion to congratulate you very dearly and to wish you all the best in your life, especially best health and success in college. But at the same time we would like to combine our congratulations with some very personal and lasting words for you.

Even though life doesn't begin for you now plainly as an adult, no, this is nevertheless the beginning of a time when you will make many decisions by yourself. And this is not easy at times, because life has thousands of faces in which you have to look in order to find your own Self. But never place yourself on the wrong side during that search, even though the fight for the maintenance of peace makes cooperation urgently necessary. The main fight has always been achieved by the Communists and they will have to keep on doing so; human history has proven that over and over again. Do not move yourself with your words and your actions to the side of those who would doubt the life of Socialism, they are bad counselors who understand nothing. One can decide only for *or against something in life – a third possibility does not exist. Never try to connect our ideals with the character of one or another human being, but always keep our goal in mind in everything that is expected of you or that you do yourself.*

These are the words that one has to understand in daily life, whether in college, together with friends, watching television, eating lunch, giving presents or even going for a walk. Because it is the simple truth that daily life contains problems both small and large, whether it be during your college time, later in your profession or in your own family.

We tried to plant our ideals in you. The bud grew to be a young shoot which valiantly started to prepare the way into life.We wish from the bottom of our hearts, that you succeed to fill out the place where you will stand one day in our society in a straight, smart and reliable way and master it for the happiness of the people beside you and also for your own personal satisfaction. However, happiness does not come without effort; you have to fight for this right every day, in your collective, amongst your friends and camerades as well as in your personal life. You have to fight, without anger, hatred or moodiness about all the things that simply must be done.

If ever you have to make an important decision in your life, remember also a bit these words, because none of them is empty of good feelings for you and your future.

Sincerely! Your parents.

I was never really sure if there was such a thing as private fulfillment. After this letter I doubted it even more. I was just about ready to give up listening to my personal desires. I decided to write down an interpretation of happiness. It was supposed to help me set my goals and become a guide for my life. I had learned that it was hardly possible to be happy while trying to fit into the social context but that it would be impossible if I attempted not to fit in at all.

The following year was filled with activities that kept me busier than ever. The college had moved to Frankfurt (Oder). We spent all our time rotating between our college obligations and the round of social activities. The days were packed with lessons, seminars, exams and the evenings were for studying. The social activities inspired and animated by the college were as much obligations as they were our 'free time'. It was called 'sensibly-designed free time'.

There were some activities which I liked, the college singing group for example. We prepared programs for social gatherings and roll-calls and spent some time on weekends practicing. My guitar-playing enabled me to have one of the leading roles in the group. This activity made me feel strong and alive. Of course most of the time we interpreted songs with a political context and had to perform for party members at congresses and other meetings.

Roll-calls were pursued weekly and at special social occasions or memorial days of which we had quite a few. All members of the college would come together outside and take their place in a certain order, class by class. This occasion was an opportunity for the director to make a short analysis of the good and less good results among us and to motivate us to keep up the good work by continuing to study harder. This was one of the public payments which we received for doing lots of activities and filling in positive class reports. We were also paid out if we were not taking certain things seriously. Since nobody was looking to be publicly embarrassed, this was one of the real motivations for getting involved on the social side.

Once in a while our singing group got to take little trips to participate in musical festivals. One of them was the annual 'Political Song Festival' in Berlin. This was an international event with countries like Chile, Mexico and Brazil sending musical representatives. Sometimes different singing groups got together at the festival to make music and to exchange songs and ideas. So quite a lot of our social activities were good fun.

In 1986 my father's collective had someone new join. At a social gathering soon after, my parents met this new couple. They exchanged pictures of their grown up children and imagined a marriage between them. They were probably more or less joking, fantasizing about the perfect marriage. Members of the Secret Service were advised to marry within the organization. They were forbidden to marry someone with western contacts. In fact, anyone who wasn't related, in some way or another, to the government, wasn't worthy.

The next morning when I got up I saw a picture in our living room that showed a young man. I asked my mother who it was. She said something to the effect that this could be a good man for me. I felt rebellious about the fact that my mother was trying to impose a boyfriend on me. I said:

"Forget it, look at this naive face. There is no way that I'm going to get involved with such a baby. Besides, I don't accept the fact that you are selecting a man for me!" I took the picture and tore it into little pieces and dropped them on the floor. Meanwhile a similar scene was happening at Horst's parents' house. There was a difference though. He liked the cute girl in the picture and was anxious to meet her. I didn't know about that.

This whole episode kept me busy thinking. Based on my earlier experiences, I thought I had come to the right conclusion about my life. That was, that I was not there to live a balanced, happy life but rather to be controlled and dictated to by someone else. This was the way I thought because I had a picture of myself as a bad girl who needed severe people around her. I needed people around who wouldn't tolerate my bad behavior and who would supervise my stubborn nature. I believed that I had to surrender to negativity, that unpleasant circumstances were proper for some-one like me.

All these thoughts were just an intuition at that time. I was not able to think things through as clearly as I can now. By going back in memory, I can relive those feel-ings. I am now able to identify the emotional condi-tions of that period, which were as negative as the inner motor driving me towards them.

When we were in college, we used to have school on Saturdays until 11 a.m. After that I would come home and sleep for an hour. One nice Saturday in springtime when I got home after school, exhausted from the week, I had a surprise. I was sleeping like a baby when the doorbell rang and pulled me out of my com-fort zone. I don't know why but my heartbeat was on the rise at once. It was as if I knew intuitively what was to come. Shortly afterwards, my mother came into my room saying that there was a young man who would like to see me. I became increasingly nervous and said, in a loud whisper:

"This can't be. What does he want here? I didn't tell him to come. Did you know about this?" My mother said that she had known he wanted to come by sometime but not that it would be today specifically. I was drowsy and confused and when I got to the mirror, I discovered that the pillow had decorated my face with lines. What an embarrassment that he would get to see me under these sleepy conditions! While I was trying to straighten my face with cold water, my father took care of the young man, chatting with him in the livingroom. My parents were obviously very pleased and excited about the brave young suitor who was showing so serious an interest in their daughter. Finally I entered the livingroom and after a hesitant welcome, my father said he would leave us alone so we could talk. I said:

"Don't do that. I don't know what I am supposed to say to him, I never met him before." This was a really weird situation, one that I was not at all prepared for. When we were alone, I asked him pointedly:

"What are you all about?" He laughed at this rebellious welcome. He didn't really know what to say himself, so I went to the radio to put on some music. Especially at lunchtime, our radio played mostly classical music and I felt it was ridiculous to listen to that right now. I turned the knob until I found some music which I thought was able to cover up this uncool situation. Our conversation was stiff but the unusual circumstances gave it a kind of spice. I then got up and opened the living room door, asking my parents what we should do next. They both came in and realized at once that there was a western channel playing on the radio. They were embarrassed:

"What are you listening to? Did you do this, Pina?" They excused themselves to their guest, saying that in that house nobody ever listened to western radio. My mother turned it quickly back to the classical music. I think it was just an act of opposition on my part, simply to make some waves in this old fashioned kind of situation. My parents suggested that all four of us go for a ride in the car. Things started to relax. We spent a pleasant afternoon walking in the nature, having coffee and icecream and getting to know each other a bit more.

I learned that he was also studying in college and would finish in the same year as me. His school was in the south of Germany and he was therefore away for several weeks at a time. He would come home twice a month for a long weekend. He was studying to be an army officer and would eventually work at the West German border. His future job depended on the needs of society in two years from then, something which we were then unable to foresee.

Over the years I had developed the belief, with the help of my father, that only soldiers were real men. Beside a soldier, any other man seemed bland to me, less strong, less respectable. That's why the fact that he was a member of the army was a pro on my list of judgements as to whether or not he might make a good husband. It was a further plus because his profession made him a suitable son-in-law for my parents in the political context. Horst was three years older than me, tall and good looking. We made an attractive couple.

All the outside conditions seemed to speak for a marriage. I can't say for sure how much we were really in love or how much we made each other fall in love based upon these sensible outside factors. On top of this, I was fairly desperate to find the man of my life, in spite of the fact that I was not yet twenty. I was afraid to let this chance slip away because I doubted I would ever find someone else who would fit so perfectly into my parents' life and mine, at the same time.

After we had known each other for about two months, I went to work in a summer-camp, taking care of a group of children. It was part of our college training. The last night before going home, I did something I had never done before. I had a brief affair. Unfortunately, as a result I had a mark on my neck and everyone was curious about it. I was very shy and felt a bit guilty. I lied about it, being afraid of trouble.

From that time on, his parents started to dislike me. I had not been honest and now I was a person not to be trusted. Their misgivings turned into outright aversion. I presume it was because of that incident but I don't even know for sure since they never spoke about it. I wasn't aware then, that this could be the key to the hatred of the following years. Not much later, Horst broke some news to me that would subsequently justify my parents' disapproval of an eventual marriage. During a dinner at a restaurant, he told me that he already had a child with another woman. He said she tricked him into this while he was drunk. Even though I found that very stupid of him, I felt we were now on an equal footing with regard to our immaturity.

Horst and I hardly knew each other at that time and we were certainly too inexperienced to take on the responsibility of marriage. Our parents were now united against our idea of getting married. These were the same people who, a short time earlier, had brought us together and they were now trying to pull us apart. All of a sudden we felt like Romeo and Juliet, who had to defend their love against angry families.

If it was not for love, then our marriage was to prove that we could make it with or without their blessing. I must say that the criticism of our parents brought us closer together. We felt we had to protect each other. My parents did not distance themselves from us as Horst's did. Each time I went to the house of my future in-laws, there was something wrong. His mother would get mad about certain things her son did, the way he mixed up his laundry for instance. Sometimes, she would get madder and madder until she was yelling hysterically. I felt so sorry for Horst. During those last weeks, I realized that he had a hard time taking any position. He seemed very insecure about everything. As I witnessed his mother's treatment of him, I understood where it came from.

At one point I ventured to defend him by telling her that she should not get mad over every little thing that her son did or did not do. She was furious with me and I had little option but to leave the house there and then. All I could do was to advise Horst to come with me. He stayed, unable to go against his mother.

Still we got married. Having been taught that I had to sacrifice my own needs to fulfill those of others people, I took it as my duty to rescue Horst from his destructive circumstances. I even felt responsible for trying to influence and correct character traits of his that would make him become a better human being. It never occurred to me that I should take care of myself first. I was told that I was the one who needed to change but, surrounded as I was by their immovable dogmatism, I was not able to do so. No more was Horst, who continued to be dominated by his mother throughout our marriage.

In the winter he took me down to the city where he was studying. He organized for me to stay with a family who were good friends of his parents. He told me everything was prepared and organized with them. I went down there and had a great time with Horst and the two kids of the family, a girl and a boy. The girl was about my age. When I returned from this short but wonderful vacation, I had an unpleasant surprise. My parents-in-law started to put me down for being what they called, dirty and irresponsible, disrespectful and undiplomatic. Before I knew what they were actually talking about I found myself in a whirlpool of unforgiveness. I finally understood that the daughter of the family we stayed with, was in love with Horst and that she hoped to make a couple with him one day. I was speechless when I heard that. I felt betrayed as well, knowing that Horst hadn't told me anything about it and now, after the event, would say no word in my defense.

I understood right away how that made me look in the eyes of his parents. I asked myself why, in this particular relationship, situations were always occurring which made me look like a monster. They called me a slut several times. Too many situations of that kind had come over me in relation with Horsts' family. I hoped that Horst would show his colors one day, telling his family to get off my back. It was tough for me to realize, even three years later, that he was not capable of supporting me. In the end, I rescued my heart from that marriage but only just in time.

When I eventually decided to get divorced it was not only a divorce from my husband. I divorced my past life at the same time. I stepped out of my pattern and had the strongest need to go ahead alone. I needed to find myself. I realized that I could not be happy being stuck in old habits and patterns without an open view on life. For me, a real sense of life means change and development. During my marriage I felt like a wild horse locked up in a small territory called 'routine'. I don't say that we did not try to be different. But the expectations of our families, especially, in this case, that of my husband, took away what little air we had to breathe.

One of the reasons why my parents-in-law didn't like me was because I was constantly asking questions and looking for answers. I ask questions about life and do not hide the fact that I want to build a life based on my own beliefs. People in our society called that being a rebel. I was nineteen at the time and trying to do the best I could. I believed that a positive attitude would enable me to give what I wanted to - love. But neither flowers nor a smile could protect me from their negative attitude. This was tough but I thought I could live with it. When it came to the point where they started to tell lies about me to my husband and the people they knew, I was no longer able to deal with it. The time of my marriage was overshadowed with me having to defend who I really was and breaking my heart on the rocks of their contempt.

Horst's parents did not come to our wedding. Instead they let us know that they had put the invitations in the

garbage pail. Their disapproval humiliated me then and it hurt my husband. He was forced to make an unfair choice. But not even that made me give up the hope of a peaceful marriage. What really destroyed me was the mistrust of my husband. Throughout the few years of our marriage I felt more as though I was on trial rather than a woman who was loved. But all this came later.
In June of 1987, there was a Summerfest organized for the people of the apartment buildings of our area. Most of these people were members of the Secret Service. It was an area reserved for members of that organization. However, it was not the very special area that some people may think. The buildings were five stories high and there was no elevator. Our area appeared to be no different from that of other apartment territories.

It was a tradition that each of these little communities organize a Summerfest. Here we had stands with beverages and things to eat. The food was mainly delicious potato salad and German sausages which I have come to miss very much in North America. The thought of going back to Germany now, makes me think straight away of the aroma and taste of these sausages, which we often ate outdoors. Anyway, besides eating and drinking, people prepared different things that they offered for sale in front of their houses. There were balloons everywhere and loud music filled the air. Many of the children participated in sports competitions. I had done so when I was smaller. We had a lot of fun.

In the evening, everybody got together for a dance which was animated by a group called Ruby. All the bandmembers worked for the Secret Service as well. From the window of my parents' apartment, I watched the group making its stage preparations. They were setting it up in the large interior square which was a feature of all the apartment blocks in that area. As I watched I couldn't help the rush of energy that I felt inside. It was pounding in my head:

"Go and say Hello. Tell them that you would like to sing in their band." Just the thought of going to say hello to total strangers made my blood race. Besides, I wore my hair in braids and I wasn't sure how they would react to the big girl trying to look cute, wanting to conquer the band. I loved to imagine myself as a singer in the band but I didn't think I could ever be so lucky. I stood there motionless, feeling a very strong impulse to go and speak to them. I should always listen to that feeling because it usually leads me to decisions that are good for my development.

My parents saw me staring at the band and they seemed to read my mind. They actually encouraged me to go and introduce myself which amazed me. They were usually so reserved on the subject of talking to outsiders or of thinking of me in the context of the music business. Still, the bandmembers were Security people.

I finally went downstairs and moved slowly towards the stage. All I could think of was how silly I must look, heading in that direction. One of the band members greeted me with a friendly word. My fears were banished at once. I told him my name and asked if they could use a second vocalist. At that stage, there was a young man doing the vocals by himself, backed up occasionally by one of the others. He answered with a simple yes and we exchanged phone numbers to make an appointment for an audition.

That was all. We spent just two minutes talking. Looking back, it's hard to believe what an impact those two minutes were to have on my artistic career! I went back upstairs as though in a dream. I couldn't believe the step I had just taken. It was my first true connection to the music scene. I was determined not to let go of it. They even offered me a chance to join a practice session! On top of all this, my mother and father told me they appreciated the courage which had led me to the day's success! I was so happy to see their attitude. It helped to calm the waves of anxiety I had been having about their eventual disapproval and enabled me to openly share my happiness with them.

A few days later I was invited to meet the band. I took my guitar with me and performed a song that was very popular at that time. Although it was a song for a duo, I managed well alone. I was hired right away. Afterwards, this same song became the favorite duet for the lead singer and myself.

None of us spoke English at that time. The singer knew a bit of the language but most of the band members were very limited. In order to make the lyrics sound original, we wrote down the pronunciation of the words and practiced them as best we could. That enabled us to sound quite English even though we didn't know what we were singing about. Naturally, we also performed a lot of German songs.

By joining this group I found another home. It made me feel more connected to life. I had left the choir by then because I was older than the maximum age of sixteen. I could have gone into the adult choir but I thought their chanting was too serious and the people a bit too old for me.

Ruby corresponded more to my need to explore and be involved with popular songs. The band did not even think of producing a record. Neither did they get any money for doing their shows. It was a band which interpreted only well-known songs. Yet there was another kind of pay. We were having fun doing something we loved. My personal pay was just in getting to perform, being able to collect some stage experience and to build some basic connections to people in the music business. This was a big thing for me at that time. It helped me to get my foot in the door.

Besides being a member of the band, I visited the Music School of the town to take classical singing lessons. I developed a very warm connection to my teacher. She enabled me to discover the real power of voice. She also encouraged me in my idea of becoming a professional singer. Besides the other members of Ruby, she was one of the few people who supported me in pursuing my artistic ambitions.

In May of 1987, just a few weeks before I got married, we had to join a camp for two weeks which was exclusively for our military and first-aid training. It was called a Civil Defense camp and was supposed to prepare us for situations of war or catastrophe where we would be able to provide some medical help. We were also introduced to some military exercises. Every day started early in the morning with a jogging tour and was continued with a military roll-call. We had to wear a uniform and fall in line, performing military greetings with one hand lifted to the forehead. The rest of the day was filled with seminars and practical exercises regarding first aid and so on. It was interesting to learn about these things although I felt strange being obliged to act and obey like a soldier.

Nothing could really interfere with my happiness about my upcoming wedding in the month of July. I was looking forward to marriage as something that would protect me from the storms of life. I imagined it as a cradle where I could hide, feeling secure and taken care off. This probably came from my feeling of being wounded, my inability to protect myself which, in the end, led me to unhappy relationships. I expected something from it that could not be, at least not until I learned to take care of myself emotionally.

Not being aware of it then, I was feeling joyous and had high hopes. I understand now that high expectations were partly the cause of my disappointment. Still, I do not want to live after the dictum that he who doesn't expect things to happen, can't be disappointed. I believe someone who doesn't have expectations has nothing to base his development on. This marriage helped me to understand at least, what it was that I did not want in life.

The only thing that added a bitter taste to my happy anticipation was the attitude of my parents-in-law. I started to have presentiments of what was coming but I was not ready to pay them any serious attention. A relationship like ours, the combination of two grownups in child-sized shoes could be easily affected by destructive attitudes from the outside and turn from a safe cradle into a nest that is vulnerable to attack.

Even though my husband-to-be was optimistic when he said:

"We'll still be able to build a nice life for ourselves," he could not hide his sadness about the inexorable attitude of his parents. No phonecall, no visit from Horst ended without him coming back with hanging shoulders and sad eyes or being drunk. He was very affected by the arguments he was constantly exposed to through his parents. As he told me, this was an old pattern that he knew all too well and he used to say:

“It’s always the same. They always find something to give me hell.” As his girlfriend, I was just another target by means of which they could express disapproval concerning their son. Because of the lack of communication, I can only guess at what their real motives were for not attending the wedding. Yet I had the impression they looked for an excuse, a reason to cover up not being there.

It is not uncommon that the family of the bride arranges the wedding. When it came to choosing the place for the party, our families faced a minor difficulty which quickly became a huge conflict and the ostensible reason for Horst’s parents not to participate at the wedding. While they wanted to celebrate in a restaurant that came closer to being a pub, my parents had selected a classy restaurant in a hotel. Horst’s parents insisted on having it their way or not at all.

Wedding in Frankfurt (Oder), July 1987

A wedding is an exciting event. Horst's parents had already done it once for their daughter but for my parents, it was going to be the first time. I feel sorry for the fact that their happy preparations were overshadowed by anxiety caused by the strange attitude of the other family. My parents did not fully approve of the fact that I was going to marry someone who had already made a baby while drunk and who obviously did not care too much about this 'mistake', since he only sent money for his child with the greatest reluctance. Yet they still supported me in my decision and wished me nothing but the best. They welcomed my husband very warmly at all times and he was treated as a respected member of our family. Meanwhile, his family gave me the feeling that I did not deserve their positive attention. For ages, I looked for the answer on my side but I came to the conclusion that these people didn't like themselves and couldn't stand anybody else much either.

Horst could not really comprehend the way his parents were acting and tried his best to commit himself fully to our relationship. In trying to untangle himself from his parents' emotional web, he became very unhappy and dissatisfied. This caused us a lot of problems and misunderstandings right from the beginning. He admitted that he wasn't able to cope with the disapproval of his parents. Even though I could understand that, I was very frustrated with the prospect of having to bring all this drama into my marriage. We already spent too much time arguing about his parents' latest device instead of building our life together. What was it going to be like after we were married?

The wedding itself was set up very nicely by my parents. After getting ready in the morning we left the house to head for the ceremony. Just when we were about to walk out the door of the apartment building, a little orchestra started to play music. That was a sweet surprise and we stood astonished in the doorway, listening to them. The music lured some people out on to their balconies to see what was happening. It was a fine start to our special day. After the brief concert, we all left for the City Hall in which the ceremony was going to be held.

Neither of us was a member of a church which is why we were going to be married in the City Hall. There was a special room there, set aside for just this kind of event. It was a lovely space, all decorated with flower arrangements. During the preparations a few days earlier, we had chosen the music we wanted to hear in the ceremony. We chose a piece by Beethoven. As far as the wedding rings were concerned, it was not as romantic as I have discovered it to be in North America. Men weren't used to surprising their girlfriends with engagement rings. At least it was so in our families. So I went to choose both rings with my father, who also paid for them.

Neither was it common to have a best man or a bride's maid so we did without. When the wedding ceremony got under way, my parents' eyes were filled with tears. I am not sure how much of it was because of the actual marriage and how much of it was caused by the missing family members.

It was not easy to accept that Horst was there all alone, without a single family member to see him through it. After the ceremony we received congratulations all round but there was a certain emptiness that could not be denied. Until the beginning of the ceremony, there had still been some faint hope that the recalcitrant pair might appear. We did not want to believe that they would follow up on such a hardhearted act, not only towards me and my family but especially towards their own son. After all we were all decent people, for the most part reasonable and there was nothing which would have clearly justified their behavior. Just in case they changed their minds, my father reserved four places for them at the restaurant but he invited two couples to fill them not long before we sat down to eat. So that was that. The other guests were members of my family: my parents, my sister, my grandmother and my uncle and aunt.

Before going to the restaurant we had an appointment in a photo studio where my husband and I were photographed by a professional. After that we went to carry out another traditional part of the ritual, as it was then in East Germany. It was common on one's wedding day to honor the Soviet soldiers who had given their lives during the liberation of Germany from fascism. Usually, the couple went to the War Memorial right after the ceremony, to lay a floral arrangement of the bride at the foot of the monument.

This rather ordinary event led to an incident which changed the course of the rest of the day. We went from the City Hall to the Memorial by car. It was a rainy day out and there was a good deal of water on the ground. One of the guests was in charge of taking photos. He was dressed impeccably in a white suit and was wearing white shoes as well. As he went to get out of the car he slipped and, just for a second, hung on with one leg on the ground and the other wildly trying to regain his footing, before he fell clean into the middle of a muddy puddle. For a moment he sat there stunned, looking around at the others, trying to comprehend the nature of the disaster which had struck him. Then as his face turn rather red with the first flush of anger, several of us broke out into involuntary laughter at the sight of him. It was far too catastrophic to be serious about!

Although this caused some momentary embarrassment, even the poor victim was soon able to make a joke out of it and he went to change after having taken the appropriate photos. Somehow this incident cheered up the whole party for the rest of the day. The oppression that had been felt before seemed to vanish and we were ready to start enjoying ourselves.

So we went to the hotel and were led into a dining room which was reserved for small parties. Everything was prepared in a very festive and cheerful way. We were placed at a big round table which was beautifully decorated. We drank champagne and had a delicious meal. Everybody seemed to enjoy themselves. Just behind the hotel was a nature park where we all went for a walk after the meal. The weather had cleared up and the sun was shining down on us. Of course we drew the attention of other people because we were all dressed up in wedding outfits. The atmosphere was now very pleasant. We had decided that we were no longer going to be affected by our absentees.

After the walk we went back inside and were now led into a small room in which we were going to spend the rest of the afternoon and the evening. In the European tradition, we had coffee and cake in the afternoon, after which my father took his accordion out and began to play music. His accordion playing is really the highlight of our family parties. I am never so happy as when he is doing that.

Since my wedding dress was cut long and tight, I had brought another white dress in which I was better able to move about. Everybody was in a real party mood by then and we all started to dance. Suddenly the door opened and a member of Ruby, the band I was in, stood there with a bunch of flowers. There is a tradition in Germany to have a big party just before the wedding. It is held at night and we invite all the people we would like to be sharing this time with. Not all of them come to the ceremony later. It is usual for every guest to bring some kind of glass that he breaks in front of the door before entering. That's why the shower is called *Polterevening*, literally, the evening when we make lots of noise by breaking or smashing things! Sometimes people come and crash a whole toiletbowl on the street! Anything is possible.

The wedding itself is then celebrated with family and relatives two days later. The day in between is used to recover from the first party and to get ready for the next. My band joined the *Polterevening* as well. That's why it was a happy surprise when one of them showed up at my wedding to congratulate me in their name.

After he left, we kept on partying and got ready for dinner. There was a big cold buffet from which we served ourselves. While we were eating our cake, my sister and I told the story of 'The Rabbit and the Hedgehog' to the guests. We used to do that when we were kids and it was fun to see that we could still do it after such a long time. At that time we had learned the words from a cassette and each played different roles. It was a welcome amusement for everybody at the table. After dinner the party went on with music and dancing. We all had quite a few drinks and I suddenly decided to demonstrate some of my judo ability. Amazingly enough, even my parents laughed and enjoyed watching me demonstrate some falls with my white dress on. The rest of the evening went by very fast.

By the end, my father had entered his melancholic state of mind. He was sitting on a chair with his accordion and had sorrowful eyes. He played and played but he did not sing anymore. Everybody's energy was winding down. It was time to go home. After waiting in vain for a taxi that had been called half an hour before, some of us decided to walk home. I was a bit disappointed that the mood was so low at the end. My mother walked in front of us and was soon out of sight. My father was still at the restaurant.

Horst and I walked together until we got into an argument about something. Suddenly, he began walking so fast that I could not follow with my high heels and I ended up walking alone through the black streets with my white dress. I arrived at my parents' place a full half hour after my husband, kissed my mother goodnight and left with Horst for our little apartment at the boarding school.

We did not talk much that night, nor did we fall asleep arm in arm. I felt sorry for this sad and unromantic ending to our wedding but I could also understand that Horst must have felt terrible after what his parents had done to him. So I cried myself to sleep. Sometimes life holds situations that are hard to accept. We wish it could be so different.

The next evening Horst left again for the army. He came back the following weekend and we left together to go camping in the north. We met two buddies of his and spent two weeks together at a campsite. It was constantly raining but we still had a lot of fun. All of us loved nature and we did a lot walking in the woods. At other times, we ate boiled potatoes under our makeshift rain-shelter or hung out in bars. We had two motorcycles which took us wherever we wanted. Sometimes we took the train to visit a nearby city. It was a good time spent together. When we came home from this rainy honeymoon, Horst had to go back to the army and my summer break from college was soon finished as well.

We were both entering our last year of college which was a big relief for me. The end of college meant the beginning of our real life together. We would get an apartment and see each other every day and not just every two weeks on the weekend. For now we had to face being separated most of the time and of course we did not really get to know each other. There was a lot of magical thinking involved in our relationship because there had not been enough real experiences from which to learn about each other. We were both in love with an ideal vision of the other and it did not even come close to being who we really were. We set out to do our best.

Our student lives continued. As in almost every social activity in our country, a prize was given to the highest achievers. Everything was directed towards finding a winner. That was supposed to be our motivation. Cultural-political programs were a permanent part of our student lives. Each class would prepare such a program including music, dance and little sketches and the jury would pick the best one. For that we got points that were good for the image of the class and worth something towards the report of the year. I spent a lot of time chasing those points.

At the end of each college year, every class had to give a yearly report, a so-called '*Fightprogram*'. It was a summary of their activities and achievements, their goals of the past year, both fulfilled and unfulfilled and their plans for the year ahead. This report was the substance around which we oriented our social lives. We got used to focussing on the outside world instead of ourselves. We were told that by performing for the society it would be good for our personal development, since we were the future of that society. To me that seemed like a strange logic, since my own development had always seemed to suffer, so that the society might be served.

I was getting closer to giving my first real lesson in school. That coincided with the period we call the '*Fooltime*', which begins on the eleventh of November each year, at exactly eleven minutes past eleven. Everybody stops whatever they are doing for a moment and makes a noise with whistles or whatever is available. In my youth we went to school with funny clothes on and walked through the streets being noisy and getting attention. You could call it a mini-Halloween.

In Germany we don't have Halloween as such. We have no decorations or big parties at that time of the year. It is in February that the real parties start, lasting for about three days. They are called the Three Crazy Days, *Rosenmontag*, *Fastnacht* and *Aschermittwoch* which fall on a Monday, Tuesday and Wednesday. Disguise and drinks are the only things that count during that time and the last of those days is the official end of *Fooltime*.

I remember one year in November, the President of Russia died just at the beginning of the *Fooltime*. Because of the solemnity of the occasion, there was a ban on the normal happy activities of the eleventh. Noone was supposed to play the fool on the streets and I recall my father criticizing me that day for attempting to have some fun anyway. By then, I was really beginning to get annoyed at the extent to which politics influenced our lives.

In preparation for this annual event, some of us girls organized a little dance-show, performing the CanCan. We made our own costumes and had a good time. Just the fact that we were unprofessional dancers made it funny in appearance, so it was perfect for the party.

Even though there was a lot to enjoy during those few days, I was struck by a certain anxiety. I was facing my first teaching lesson the following day, in a real school class. I would have twenty little kids in front of me. Just thinking about that gave me the shivers. I was still thinking that I was not where I was meant to be.

Next morning, I had to find all my courage to master this new challenge. I was afraid of the kids and very nervous. Everything went as planned except that I had the greatest difficulty understanding what the kids were saying. They were about nine years old and I had never really had any contact with that age group. I spent my morning feeling embarrassed because I had to keep repeating, "I beg your pardon?"

My own teacher and the rest of our group were also attending the lesson and in the analysis afterwards, they told me that I had done pretty well. However, I had had a different impression. When I got home, I cried my eyes out and wrote a poem about what an impossible teacher I was going to be. Later on I came to a conclusion about that first day's class. It wasn't so much the way it had gone that had affected me as it was what I was doing. I just did not want to teach.

There were some other ways in which we did things for society. We used to organize frequent Solidarity Bazaars. We would produce little handworked items, souvenirs and such, as well as baked cakes. Then we sold these things and put the money into a special bank that was only for Solidarity purposes. The money would go to countries with special needs, such as those with a high rate of starvation or where the people were suffering from wars or natural disasters.

Once in a while we had to do a '*Subotnik*', meaning in russian 'work on saturday'. We would take over a certain territory of the city or maybe our college building and give it a big clean up. Sometimes we would just take special care of it for a certain period of time. Sports contests under the flag of our country were also common. Prizes for the winners were named after important political figures of the past. Poetry contests were another way of being socially active. Each class had a committee of about five students who were in charge of different subjects. One was the President of the class, another the Vice-President and the other three were responsible for Culture, Political Development and the Treasury.

For two years I was responsible for the Political Development of the class. I was called the Class Propagandist. Each month I organized a special hour during which I would talk about the political history of our country. Once a week I animated a discussion about the political situation in our country and important happenings elsewhere in the world. It was hard to make it interesting since most of the students were obviously tired of politics altogether. Still those talks were important as far as the Annual Class Report was concerned and they were always supervised by a teacher. We made a report of the themes we discussed. I remember the subject of one of them was:

> *'National Pride. Are we ashamed to be revolutionary? Is a person appreciated if he or she accomplishes something for the society?'*

I liked the subject of this seminar because it expressed the awareness of a problem in our society which was starting to become clearer and clearer. It expressed the doubts people were having about the continuing value of socialism. It was just not cool to be 'red', any longer. It made those of us who defended socialism become, unofficially, outsiders or black sheep. The official authorization of this theme was, I think, one important step towards facing the new reality. It was something which, in the past, had not been done enough in the GDR.

Each year we had to participate in an examination in

order to demonstrate our political knowledge. We were given a medal called 'For good knowledge', in either gold, silver or bronze, our performance having been judged by a jury. The jury was made up of teachers and students. The teachers also had a committee which was in charge of supervising all the different goings-on. Then there was a further committee representing all the students together at the college. Only the best and, politically-speaking, most reliable students were chosen to join that group. The jury was the quintessence of socialist leadership. Our society was such a complex system. Everything had its place, everything was under control.

In our country we had an organization called the German-Russian Friendship Society. We were obliged to join this organization just as we had to join a union called Free-German Youth in grade eight in high school. These organizations all held regular meetings during which we would talk about our political activities. We discussed how we intended to develop the friendship with our Russian brothers and sisters, with the intention of strengthening both societies. We also paid small monthly fees for every organization that we were in and had to fill our membership books with stamps to prove that we were up to date. This was taken very seriously by the system.

The 7th of October was our National Day. The army used to parade in Berlin to demonstrate the power of the GDR. As a member of the army, Horst participated in the parades. It was a special occasion and I was proud to see him in this procession of power. At this time of my life, my mind was still imbued with the political correctness of our system, including its military side.

Family members and other citizens would stand on the side of the road, exulting in the parade and winking at the marching soldiers. Little children would swing paper flags and carry balloons to express their excitement. During the whole of the day and evening our two TV channels would be filled with images of these activities, showing happy faces and laughing children sitting on their fathers' shoulders. All this together seemed to be a proof that the country and its people were a unit. That is what the government intended.

It was no different on the 1st of May, the day of the workers. We were not asked to join the yearly march through the city streets; we were obliged to. It was organized by the government and concerned schools, workers' collectives in factories, sportsclubs, indeed all organizations within the society. That meant that, all the way down the line, everybody had to show up. The long stream of people headed towards a big podium where political representatives and the deputies of our city would stand and receive the hurrahs and enthusiastic smiles of the multitudes, as they passed in front of them. We carried posters with slogans like, '*We love our country*', '*We support the working class all over the world*' and so on.

In the first years of school, we were still quite excited about the large number of people on the streets. It was like a big party for us. As we got older we noticed the severity that was expressed when someone tried to be excused from participating in these marches. From then on we behaved in a more rebellious fashion, realizing that there was a lot of artificial enthusiasm that was created by obliging everyone to participate. The same phenomenon occurred at political manifestations such as the Memorial Day for the victims of fascism.

No matter what the weather was like, we all had to meet at a large square where we would listen to the speaker on a platform. He would confirm for one long hour how important it was to maintain peace. Even though the intention was very positive, we became more and more disinterested over the years, for the simple reason that we were bored by lectures which were always the same, year in and year out.

Obviously, that was not the concern of the government. The important thing was that we were there so the officials could inscribe one more successful result in their political agenda. It was not the quality that counted but the number of participants. The government seemed to have little confidence, being afraid of disapproval from their own people. They closed their eyes to the fact that significant numbers of people had to be more or less ordered to these occasions. They made themselves believe that everything was going great. They wanted to have many listeners, so they made sure a lot of ears would be present.

We were so sheltered from knowing anything about the positive side of capitalism or the negative side of our own system that it was almost a sensation when our college received a delegation from France, which came to exchange knowledge about school structures in the two countries. They had been invited to our city by the government and were joined by a translator who made it possible for us to communicate. The meeting was carried out in a very official way, starting with the fact that we met in a conference room. The formal atmosphere made everything appear very serious.

Some of the students had prepared questions concentrating on theoretical contents. So we sat there, under the surveillance of several teachers and asked a selection of the driest questions. Even though several of us had prepared some more interesting topics, the tension was such that we didn't even think of mentioning them. I could feel the oppression amongst us when we were asked if there were any extra questions. Secretly I was bursting to speak out but I was too shy. I didn't say anything during the whole meeting. All I was really interested in was to know what their life was like over there but that was obviously beside the point.

Still, I was very surprised to learn how complex their school system seemed to be, with private schools and public schools, and many possible directions available within the first ten years of schooling. In our system everybody went to the only kind of school that existed, the Polytechnical Superior School.

For me the members of this capitalist delegation were something like aliens. It was not so much the fact that they looked different because they really didn't. I had expected to notice some abnormality, based on what I was taught about the West but it wasn't obvious. Nevertheless, they seemed to be wrapped up in some kind of secret and I had the impression I was having my first encounter with beings from another sphere.

Frankfurt (Oder), Fall 1987

Our college building was downtown while our boarding school was in another part of the city. We travelled back and forth on the street-trolley which is a very common form of transport in Europe. The boarding school looked similar to a normal apartment block. In the entrance-way was a little office which was occupied by a couple of students. They carried out the job of security guards. Each of us had our turn at being on guard duty. Considering the large number of students, this was not a big commitment. Yet it was a regular part of our student life.

We had to do shifts of six hours, sometimes at daytime, sometimes at nighttime. After a night shift we were dismissed from school until about two o'clock in the afternoon. All of us had a student pass that we had to show to the guards upon entering. The pass also allowed us to buy reduced fares for the street-trolleys and to visit shows, museums, theaters and so on, for free or at a reduced price.

In the Fall, I started the practicum at a real school. This was a period during which all the final-year students had to get into teaching for real. We each had a class to take care of with the help of a mentor and we worked with them just as we would do in one year's time, on our own. I had a hard time. Many others enjoyed it a lot because they could not wait to finally do some real teaching. Many of them felt that the college program was too theoretical and didn't concentrate enough on the practical aspects of teaching. I didn't rush to get to that point. I was afraid of schools and I wondered at times if it did not have something to do with the anxious time I had had in school as a kid. Even the sound of the school bell still made me nervous.

After the first few lessons it was not difficult for me to stand in front of a class and I managed to get a bit into the spirit of being a teacher. I even succeeded in building a good relationship with the eight year olds but even so, I did not feel truly comfortable with it all. I could not really get the satisfaction out of it I was looking for.

The practical part lasted for three months. It was our final preparation before we could go out into the world as professional teachers. I felt much aversion towards the normal activities of a teacher, such as preparing lessons at home for the next day and making psychological evaluations of the pupils. I could not convince myself that I should feel joy and fulfillment doing this.

I often put the preparation off until late at night. Even though I was sometimes still working in the early hours of the morning, it appeared I was giving great lessons. The theoretical part was no problem for me but I could not feel the fire I thought a dedicated teacher needed to feel if he or she wants to truly succeed. Inside of me burned another fire. At the time I thought it was just a negative feeling but I realized soon after that it was the true flame of what I really wanted to be. I didn't know how it would turn out yet but I couldn't think of anything else than being an artist.

Of course it is normal to have certain difficulties in the learning process. It takes patience and hard work to overcome the hurdles at the beginning but that was not my problem. The conflict which I had faced at the time when I was more or less squeezed into this profession, came up again very strongly. I finally sat down in the middle of the night and formulated, on three pages, my request for ex-matriculation from college. Again I had reached a point where I was no longer willing to wear a mask of submission towards the will of my parents and the society. I stood up for what I wanted to do and that was, inevitably, music.

I felt incredible relief after giving my resignation to the director of our college. I was able to face the remaining few days of the practicum with much more optimism, knowing that I was leaving what was, to me, a heart-oppressing field.

I finished the practicum with very good results and was now invited to see the director in person. He was very popular with us because of his warm personality and open attitude. He was a man of progress and support for others and not a person of judgements or automatic procedures. That's why I had a lot of faith in giving my resignation to him. He tried to explain to me that it was in my interest to finish college. He told me that nothing in life was written in concrete, in the sense that a human being would sooner or later find his way towards his real destination.

He said that my college degree would be a support on my way in life rather than a hindrance. He could very well understand my artistic ambitions, for he felt sympathetic about my performances within cultural programs at the college. He also drew my attention to the possibility that, in later years, my husband could hold this step against me as a sign of weakness. He suggested that that might end up making me very unhappy. He further asked me what would be the better choice: to have struggled for three and a half years and come out of it without a paper, or to struggle a few more months and finish with a degree. I had to admit that I was losing much more by stopping now instead of just taking the last few steps.

In the end, he suggested I go to another institution after college where I could qualify myself as a music teacher for all age groups in school. It was an act of kindness, his trying to help me out in that way. He could see that I was feeling trapped into giving math and German lessons for the rest of my life. I also told him that I did not want so much to teach music as to make music myself. Anyway, he said all these nice things in a way that convinced me that I was studying for my development and not for anybody else's. That was something I needed to hear because part of my biggest frustration was the feeling of having to please everybody except myself.

I went out of his office with a great feeling of being respected. That's what I call being a pedagogue. He really got to me and I felt energized and strong enough to face the last six months of college. I continued to study but was now looking for a way to get around the obligation that I had to work at least three years in a school after college.

It was so easy to get caught up in the system and become surrounded by mistrust and mental terror. During my time in college, I had periods where I desperately wanted to change the direction of my profession from being a teacher to studying music. I believed that it was unwise to just go to officialdom and ask about the possibilities of taking such a step. So I thought of another way to do it, by means of which I might be able to protect myself.

I had heard about women staying at home to be housewives and I thought it would be harmless enough to go and seek information, pretending that was my intention. I went to the administration building of our city, where I asked for the person in charge. I asked her if it would be possible for me to stay home after college in order to raise a family. She got upset and was raising her voice only two minutes after I entered her office. I was shocked by her reaction. I grew afraid. She got personal very fast, saying things to me like:

"What is going on in your mind? If you don't work now you'll never learn how to work." It's not so much what she said but more the way she talked down to me. I said that my husband would make enough money to support a family. She got more upset with every word. She said I was lazy and irresponsible. I suddenly felt as I used to feel when my father talked at me. I started to cry. What kind of trouble had I gotten myself into. This was all a terrible misunderstanding and I felt the need to justify myself. I finally told her the truth saying that my real intention was to study music, that I was trying to find a way out of the education system. She was too busy being angry to listen further. I left the office feeling completely intimidated by what had happened. I could hardly believe I had received such harshness.

Looking at it today, I believe that was partly what my parents were trying to protect me from. They used to tell me:

"You're going to have a hard time if you don't follow the path, so don't complain or try to make changes." I guess I haven't learned this lesson yet and can't see myself doing so.

Every week at the city court, there was a public consultation hour so that people could get answers concerning the law and the rights of citizens. This is where I went to get information as to whether or not I could switch to another field immediately after college. The man there wanted to have my name and address. He told me it was the normal procedure. Since I wanted to stay anonymous he was unable to give me any information. So I went to the city library instead and looked up the law books by myself, hoping to find a loophole that would allow me to slip quietly out of the teaching profession. There had to be a way.

It hardly seems to be a coincidence that I got pregnant at that time. It really looked like it was planned so I would not have to work after college but it was not so. At least it was not consciously planned for that purpose. We just wanted to have a child. It was nothing out of the ordinary to marry young and have kids but in my case, it was going to lead me on a path towards a destination other than teaching. I did not know that then because nobody foresaw the changes in society which were soon to come. Had the social circumstances remained as they were, I would have had to work in school for at least three years at the completion of my year at home with the baby.

I was three months pregnant with Jan, when a major artistic opportunity occurred out of the blue. The wife of one of the bandmembers had professional contacts with artists and producers in the music business. As a result she was able to recommend me to someone who was looking for a female singer. I was to be one of the vocalists on a single track. It was a chance too good to miss and I didn't hesitate. It was such a nice change from the dull time I was having in college. We did the recording in a studio near Berlin and afterwards I knew, deep down that that was what I most wanted to be doing.

I was getting several visits a week from members of Ruby, who came to pick me up and take me to band practice. The girls at school kept looking at me curiously, wondering at the truth. Since I never talked about my musical activities, they didn't know who the people were or what we were doing. Since it didn't occur to me to set the record straight, they could only guess at the nature of our relationship. Unbeknownst to me, they were doing more than guessing.

This false impression sat festering for only a short time before Horst confronted me with the accusation that I was having an affair. I suppose that he could hardly help being suspicious. He knew the band members as well as I did and he tried to put the thought that one of them might be my lover, aside. Still he could not free himself of the doubt that I might be being unfaithful to him. When I asked him where he had got the idea that something was wrong, he told me straight out that it came from some of my classmates. That sums up the atmosphere in which I lived at that time, in college. If you weren't part of the gang then the gang was against you.

One Saturday I came home and my family received me with flowers. A rush of happiness came over me and I wondered what this sudden sign of appreciation could be for. Then they told me that they had heard *my* song on the radio and expressed how proud they were of me. I was on a total 'high' about this news. I was even more excited looking at the proud faces of my family. It gave me a good feeling of hope that my parents were not completely closed to my idea of being an artist. Yet, I also understood that they granted their emotional support only in sight of success.

In college I still kept silent about what I was doing in my free time. I didn't mention that I was singing in a band or that I had been in a studio to help record a song that was now playing on radio. I felt that I shouldn't trust my confidences to anybody and the only place where I felt secure and comfortable was with artists. We communicated well, probably because we shared something important: our passion for music. We knew about the crying of the soul and the exuberance of the mind.

I remember a situation where I pretty much withdrew from socializing with my class mates. It was Christmas time in 1987. As in every other year, we organized a Christmas party within our class. All of us prepared a little present for some member of the class. We created lovely looking gift boxes which were wrapped up with considerable warmth and affection. For my part, I had prepared quite a surprise for one of the others. The gifts were handed over one by one and there was much excitement in the room as they were opened. Suddenly, the person distributing them hesitated, holding another gift in her hand. For a moment it was so silent in the room that it seemed everyone had stopped breathing. We were all staring at a needy looking little package, rolled up in some beige paper that is normally used for mailing parcels. It was held together by a simple cord.

It was a situation that at once disturbed the harmony of the moment. It caused us to move our heads lower on our shoulders, as though we were recoiling from a painful scene. Everyone sat stolidly in their chairs, waiting to see whose name was written on that pitiful package. The girls who already held gifts in their hands drew a long breath, knowing that it couldn't be for them. Then the name echoed through the room:

"For Pina. For Pina. For Pina." The shame I felt made me wish to sink down through the floor. For a moment it occurred to me that I would discover some wonderful contents inside, that the outside was just a joke to surprise me. I opened the paper and found two colorless towels and a chocolate bar. I came close to tears. I thought that couldn't be it, there must surely have been a mistake, a misunderstanding. But the message could not have been clearer:

"I don't like you." The worst part was that everyone looked at me without a comment. I thought that there might be some words of comfort or some kind of confirmation that this was not appropriate but nobody said a thing. I couldn't help but feel that they were relieved, thinking:

"Aah, it's just her...let's see how she reacts..." I tried to smile and produced a croaking:

"Thank you." I was completely down and shocked. I soon left the party, to which I didn't seem to belong anyway. I wish I could have stood up and said that there was no point for me to accept that 'gift'. Yet, I was kind of shocked that this actually happened and that my low level of confidence allowed people to treat me like that. I felt helpless in the face of this rejection and I believed I had no other choice than to accept what I was given.

It is easy to walk all over people who are vulnerable. There is not much resistance, just a lot of pitiful acceptance towards being victimized. I thought someone might pull me up out of my pain one day by telling me that everybody was unfair to me. Instead I learned that I will continue to be hurt as long as I allow myself to be hurt. I want to teach my child not to accept the role of a victim but to take his place as any human being should, with the same rights as others. I know that I can only achieve that by helping him to be aware of his strengths and making him feel appreciated and wanted.

My parents' house wasn't too far from the boarding school. After the shock of the present-giving, I could not stay at school that night. I needed to be somewhere else. As I walked back home, I wanted to cry out all the hurt I felt. I was wandering slowly on the sidewalk when a car suddenly stopped beside me. There was a man in the car asking me if I knew of a cafe nearby.

I explained the way to him and started to move on. He asked me if I would like to join him for a coffee. I refused his offer in as friendly a manner as I could, considering the state of my emotions. I could not fight a feeling of great discomfort. Even though I told him that I had to go he still insisted. I finally turned away from the car altogether. I did not feel like being bothered after all that had happened. I wanted to hide in my cradle and know nothing of the world. The stranger put his car in reverse and slowly rolled beside me while I walked. I got really nervous, telling him to leave me alone. He was insistent. I walked on, faster and faster. He still tried to convince me to accompany him. Without stopping, I said:

"No. No, I won't. Leave me alone." Finally, he gave up and drove away. I was mixed up and unable to make sense out of these situations which came over me so unexpectedly. Nevertheless, my head had been clear enough to think of looking back and taking the number of his car. I thought he might be a criminal who was trying to trick people into his car in order to harm them and I decided to tell my father about it. Actually, this situation served to pull me out of my sorrowful state and my thoughts started to become alive again after the recent disappointment.

All of a sudden, a memory flashed through my mind like lightning:

"I know that man!" I remembered where I had seen him for the first time. It was several weeks previously, at the train station where I had been waiting for my husband. He was coming home from college for the weekend.

It was a cold and humid winter evening with snow and rain falling. It was just like the evening coming home from the Christmas party. Standing at the train station, people had the collars of their coats pulled up high against the cold, their faces searching for signs of the approaching train. I stood there feeling the chill but was happy in the expectation of seeing my husband.

Suddenly an unknown man moved towards me and started a conversation. Actually it was more of a questionnaire. He pretended that his intention was innocent, just a harmless talk to make the time go by. He asked me who I was waiting for. I saw nothing wrong with telling him. In fact, I was proud that my husband studied at a military college. When I saw that he wanted to know more I became suspicious. He asked me about the geographical position of the military buildings. He even asked me if I would take photographs of the place for him. I thought I must be involved with a western spy. A strange feeling came over me and I quickly put a stop to the conversation which I didn't feel comfortable with at all.

Fortunately the train was arriving. I looked out for my husband and pulled him away the minute I got hold of him. He wanted to know what it was all about and, quite out of breath, I told him about the man who had questioned me on military matters. At first my husband was upset by the story but he seemed to forget about it fast enough. I told my father all about it because my sense of patriotism told me I should do so.

I should have known that I was going to let myself in for another lecture about my personal instability. These people, so he instructed me, only went for the weakest members of society, from whom they could be sure of getting information. His demeanor showed that he did not appreciate the fact that I was amongst this class of weaker types. It didn't do me any good when I told him that I had turned away from the man as soon as he started to question me about specific things. My mother tuned into the discussion, saying that it was the open-hearted look on my face which acted like an invitation for people to interrogate me.

I was a bit disappointed. Somehow I had hoped for a certain protection from my parents' side. Soon the incident seemed forgotten and life had taken its usual course. Until that evening where the stranger crossed my way for the second time.

Since my father now had the number of the license plate he was able to find out about the person. The news that my father broke to me a few days after shook me and made me feel very insecure. He told me that the person in question was working for the Secret Service, the very same organization my parents worked for. The man had been ordered to check on my trustworthiness and to see if I was joining any illegal organizations or participating in any actions which might harm the country. I couldn't believe it! Me, who had spent so much time and effort in supporting the society, was now being spied on to find out how harmful I eventually might be for the system?

My understanding about situations of the past now became clearer. That's why I had been refused permission to join the Communist Party. I asked myself why I should be so important when I had no contacts with and no influence over anyone at all. Only today do I understand that this personal attention I was given had nothing to do with my being important in some way. It was simply the case that nobody's private life was free from the sharp eyes of the Secret Service. It drove me nuts.

It had started in the summer of 1985, just a few weeks after I met my first boyfriend. I was seventeen years old. As usual, my father checked out all the contacts I made. That was not a lot of work since I didn't know many people. He warned me that this 'individual', as he referred to people who were not a hundred percent 'clean', was not the ideal connection for me. He was known to be a 'weak element'. Translated into normal language, that really meant a person who had a head of his own.

I was especially amazed to hear that since the boyfriend in question was serving in the army. I was not used to hearing negative comments about army people. However, I could partially understand because I knew his point of view and his rebellious attitude towards the system. It was always a sore point with my boyfriend that my parents worked for the Secret Service. Nor did he like the way I sometimes defended them. I now have a much clearer picture about other weird situations that I had no explanation for, until the day I learned that I was being checked-up on.

One day I went to the beach by myself and not long after I was approached by a stranger. He was a good looking fellow of about thirty years of age. He opened the conversation saying that he knew me as a nurse from Hungary. I had a good laugh but he seemed so sure. These people were so manipulative that they could convince you of anything. They were ready, in the first instance, to make me believe that I was a danger to the country, so why not a Hungarian nurse!

The fellow finally had to admit that he must have been mistaken and I expected him to go back to his place. So he did but shortly after he came back and repeated to me, that he was certain that I was the nurse he had seen in Hungary. I started to get annoyed. I had never been to that country. However, the contact was made and he did not seem to be willing to let go of it. Of course I thought he was trying to cruise me. Why should I have thought that he was trying to screw me under the orders of the Secret Service. So I made sure he knew about my boyfriend, with whom I was very much in love at the time. This subject appeared to interest him immensely. I didn't feel I was being interrogated. I was rather happy that there was somebody who seemed to share my happiness.

It was the kind of conversation where you talk about life and the world, exposing opinions and different points of view. That was something that I missed very much in my life, conversations in which I felt I was actually an equal participant. The weather was beautiful and we spent three days talking and walking on the beach. He never made an attempt to come close to me, it seemed that both of us were having a good time just talking.

In the meantime, I always carried my boyfriend's letters in my handbag. They were the only things of his I had while he was away at the army. When I was alone I read them over and over again. The paper was oily from the suncream on my hands and they looked like they were ten years old already. I preferred that to not having them near me. I was totally into this falling-in-love thing. My longing to visit him became stronger and stronger. One day, when I had finished at the beach, I spontaneously decided to hitchhike to Berlin where his regiment was located. I had never gone to see him there before but I had the address from the envelope on the letter.

My naivete was going to reach its peak. I took my handbag, put on my miniskirt and a T-shirt, which were the only things I had with me, and was soon on my way to Berlin. I knew that it took about an hour and a half by car to reach the capitol from my hometown. The first time I raised my arm a car with two men in it stopped. As I got in, I saw the fellow from the beach pass by with his bicycle. He knew about my plans and winked to me. The two men were very friendly, so friendly that they offered to take me to Berlin and to bring me back home after my visit! Before doing that, they said, we should all go and have dinner.

Wasn't that a bit too much to be just a case of good luck or an act of friendliness? That's what I was asking myself only two years later. At the time, I didn't think much about it. After a nice dinner in a restaurant we headed towards the city. When we arrived at the barracks, the men said they would wait in the car for my return. The guards looked at me suspiciously but they called my boyfriend for me. He was surprised to see me and the fact that I was showing up out of the usual visiting hours gave it a touch of rebellion that he seemed to appreciate. I had the feeling that I was going up on his respect scale. He was astonished about my story of the two strangers who had brought me here and who were willing to take me back home. He couldn't help being a little suspicious of their motives but nor did he care too much. He was of a frivolous nature and he had decided not to take life too seriously in that country of ours.

He was one of those who had to go through the army in order to have a better chance of entering a university one day. His dream was to study photography and he could not stand the army. To him it was a herd of blockheads who did nothing but creep in the direction they were told to. Since he was not a person of hidden opinions it was not hard for the officials to classify him as a so-called 'weak element' of the society.

Although I didn't know it, I was going to be put into that category, as well.

A few weeks before I had gone to a dance organized by the firm of my parents for all the teenagers of the people who worked there. It was to take place in a hall just outside the Security building and the only obvious connection to it,was a door and a fire-ladder. It seemed to me that from up there one could probably look into the yard of the Security building. We were not served with alcoholic beverages, so my idea of climbing that ladder rose from pure curiosity about what would happen and what I would see if I went up there.

I had brought my best friend with me to the dance. She was my boyfriend's sister and I had actually met him when I visited her at home. I told her about my plan. She was very excited but tried at once to talk me out of it. I couldn't let it be. It seemed to be a chance for a real adventure which was too tempting to miss. While she checked the door to the dance hall to warn me if anyone approached, I quickly climbed the ladder.

When I reached the last step, I leaned my arms on the roof and looked around proudly like the discoverer of some new land. It was far less romantic than that however, for I could only see a few army trucks and offices. I didn't get a very good look either, because there was a watchtower just across the way. In it I could see a guard standing, with a gun over his shoulder. When he turned around and saw that there was someone looking at him from across the roof, his jaw dropped. I smiled at him, curious to see what he would do. His face showed he was very upset and he started making wild gestures, telling me to get myself back down, quick.

It crossed my mind that he might point the gun at me and with a friendly wink, I rushed down the ladder twice as fast as I had gone up. I think this must have been one of the rare times that a guard had something to do in that well-protected area. When I returned to the dance hall, I expected to be called to account but besides some very quizzical looks from the people in charge, nothing happened, or so I thought.

When I got home my parents already knew about my prodigious action. They were disgusted by the fact that it was their daughter who had provoked the displeasure of the firm. Especially since they were always anxiously looking out to be obedient and set a good example for everyone else. This situation was very unpleasant for them compared to those of ten years earlier. Then they had been able to laugh about my putting out the medals and taking the fifty marks.

My parents could see no reason to laugh at all after hearing the news of my prank on the ladder. Besides lecturing me about the need to take life more seriously now that I was almost eighteen, they felt completely embarrassed in my name.When they returned from work the next day, they said that they were ashamed of me because all their colleagues had heard the news within already. I was sorry to have caused them such trouble. The incident took forever to be forgotten. It could even have been a very good cause for opening a file about me at their company. Now that I was involved with this boyfriend of mine, it seemed to be reason enough for them to believe that we made a potentially 'dangerous' couple and had to be watched over.

My visit to the regiment did not last very long since we didn't feel too comfortable meeting in a room which was so cold and had such harsh neon lighting, that it turned any romance into twaddle. At least I succeeded with my surprise, leaving him feeling flattered that I had undertaken such an enterprise just to see him. And I was happy that I had managed to accomplish something that I really wanted - to kiss my boyfriend.

As I found my way back to the car, it crossed my mind that the men might have left without me but no, they were still where I had left them, patiently waiting. They kept their promise to take me back home. I arrived without problems, happy about my little adventure.

Frankfurt (Oder) 1988

Finally we headed towards our final exams in college in June of 1988. I was now six months pregnant and feeling a motivation about life that I had not experienced before. I finished all my exams with results that I would not have dreamed of. The thought of finishing college, becoming a mother and starting a family of my own filled me with pride and optimism. Then it was time for the graduation party. All I wanted was to receive my paper and get out of there. All the students acted like a family but I had never managed to make myself part of it. Now when it was time to say good bye it was too late to try to belong to them. I was on my own.

The parents of all the students were sitting in the back of the hall, attending the ceremony. I felt so uncomfortable that it brought me close to tears. All I longed for was to put it behind me and to get on with my life. After it was over, our parents received us with flowers and congratulations. My parents had accompanied me and they wanted to stay in the hall and chat. My tears were fighting their way up and I told them to come outside with me, away from all this.

Outside I could no longer hold back the tears. They helped me to release the incredible tension I had built up over the years of doing something against my will. It was finally over. My parents asked if I was crying because I should have had better results. They were surprised when I said that I was unhappy about what I was being rewarded for. They were a little less surprised when they heard that I would have preferred to study music instead. Finally it was over and I was looking forward to the next stage of my life.

My tears were also misinterpreted by others as reflecting an unhappy test. That was my fault of course because I had told noone about how well I had passed. I might have guessed that my mother-in-law would somehow get to know about it! I don't know from whom she obtained that wrong information, since I was not welcome in their house. My husband still went there alone when he was home and I was getting fed up to see him coming back afterwards, having just obtained the latest disgraceful news concerning his wife.

Over and over again, it destroyed the trust that we had been building. There would be a period of growing together, then he would see his parents and all of it would be undone. We would have to start the process all over again. Being very pregnant by then, I was no longer willing to accept it. Since I could not keep my husband from seeing his parents, I simply asked him not to tell me any of the things they were saying about me. I needed peace and harmony more than ever.

Since college was finished, we could not keep our little apartment in the boarding school. Horst was also finishing his stint at the army college but we still didn't know to which city he was going to be posted. During that time, I stayed with my parents and my husband stayed there as well, when he came back on weekends.

To get an apartment was not an easy matter. In East German society, there was no private business which organized that. We could not just go and check the housing market to choose a place to live. Everything was distributed by the government upon request. To be married made it a bit easier and to have a child was an added advantage.

To have parents who worked for the Secret Service didn't help. I think if my parents had wanted to arrange something they could have done so but they never used their position to get personal advantages. That made them different from most of the members of their organization. So it was very complicated to find a place and we only did so at the last minute. Until then we just had to go day by day, waiting for Horst's place of work to be clarified. I was getting more and more nervous about not knowing where we were going to live or whether we would have an apartment at all. I was due to have my baby two months from then. With two tiny bedrooms, my parents' place was much too small for all of us. I expressed my fears and displeasure to my family about the situation but they could do nothing about it. As for Horst's superiors, the ones in charge of it, they just took their time.

My mild criticism prompted my father to start on his usual line that this would be a good test of my character. In the past, I had had enough of my father telling me about my bad character. I told him that I didn't care who knew how I felt about certain procedures of the state. To me it seemed perfectly obvious that certain things didn't function at all well. My father went on and on about the same subject of me not being good enough. He told me:

"I despise people who only nag and do nothing, who are passionately in love with criticizing . . . I mean people like you." Tired and sad, I wrote a couple of desultory lines in my diary:

"Well, up to here I have done nothing, only graduated from High school and college with good marks. I am married and pregnant. I am twenty."

One day we got an unbelievable invitation. Horst's parents invited both of us for an ice cream. I was more than happy to go for I saw a chance to spend some pleasant time together which could be the beginning of a better relationship.

Everything did go well. His mother told me not to wait too long to have the next baby, though I had not yet given birth to the first. That didn't affect me much at all, although I might have liked to tell her to mind her own business. Nor was I bothered by the fact that my husband and father-in-law were drinking schnapps in the early afternoon. I was just happy that we were getting together.

On the way home from that first friendly encounter, we found ourselves waiting at a streetcar stop. We were talking about the arrival date of our baby when Horst suddenly said:

"Now you are trying to make me believe that I am the father of this kid!" The accusation hammering in this sentence made me dizzy. I thought I was at the end of my limits. Why was it that every time there was any kind of contact with his parents, Horst would become so hostile towards me. I couldn't stand the pain this was causing me. Probably it had to do with him not being able to deal with the conflict that existed between his parents and ourselves. Not to mention the extra problem of him being away most of the time.

The mistrust contained in that statement broke something inside of me. I suddenly felt all alone with my baby. I was not able to feel close to my husband for quite some time. I lived as in a dream, thinking that it couldn't be real, that it had to be some kind of nightmare. The dream-castle I had fashioned for us around our perfect little family had already begun to develop cracks from the constant accusations his parents had been making. To hear such a thing from his own mouth made my world fall apart. In my diary I wrote:

> *"How romantic I visualized it, to be in love! How many tears must a girl shed until she is able to laugh about true love as an unrealistic dream? I believe that goes very fast. First there is simple disappointment, then there is bitter laughter which tries to cover it up.*
>
> *Anyways, I have to stay strong now for my child as well as myself. I'll see what*

happens. What did I imagine in the first place? A huge WHY is hanging over me. I feel like a child looking with frightened eyes at the favorite vase of its mother which it has just broken, being amazed that such a thing was even possible. I have to find out if it is all due to powers which we can't control. I never want to become a bitter and cynical housedragon. At least that is how I see the women who speak with young girls about love.

My mom once said to me that there was a time when she thought as I do now. But she had to be reasonable about her inability to change the world and finally decided to accept married life as it was. Today the word marriage tastes really bitter to me, like something threatening which does not allow for any sensitivity, only tough fighting."

Life took its course and we were finally given an apartment. My parents planned to visit it with me but on the evening before, my father and I got into an argument again. The next day, he refused to drive us to the place, which was about two hours by car from our hometown. I was now almost nine months pregnant and my mother and I decided to take the train and not let father be the king over our activities.

We pursued the plan and protested, as a unit for once, against his destructive ways. My husband was stuck at college, as usual. It took my mother and I about four hours to get to the new town. To find the apartment was another couple of hours' search. There were no buses or street cars around and taxis were hard to find. We had to walk all the way and when we finally stood in front of the apartment block, I was pretty disappointed.

Our apartment was at one end, on the first floor. This meant that it would be colder in winter, since there was no apartment under or beside it. Inside, it was dirty and badly lit. All of the apartments were heated with coal. There was no central heating or hot water system as I had been used to at my parents'. All heat had to be produced by putting coal in the ovens of each of the four rooms, the bathroom, kitchen, living room and bedroom.

For the first time in my life I was obliged to do as many others still had to do, go downstairs to get my coal. I remember going down in the semi-darkness, not knowing what I might find there. A tiny window let in a small amount of light, enough to identify the coal cellar and put the key in the lock. There were lamps on the walls but they were nearly always broken. Fortunately for me, it was Horst who went most of the time. The one advantage of living downstairs was that we didn't have to carry the coal buckets all the way up from the basement to the fifth floor.

I tried to be positive and said to my mom that yet

another strong point of the place lay in its being so close to Berlin. It only took an hour and a half by bus and train to get to the big city. Anyway, it wasn't as if we had another choice. We had to take what we were offered. Still, we could see it wasn't going to be easy to make this place habitable.

The following weeks were filled with going back and forth in between the two cities. The birth date was coming closer and closer and I felt sorry that I couldn't fully participate in setting up the apartment. I was very grateful for the support of my parents who, together with my husband, cleaned the apartment and put up new wall paper and so on. They also supplied us with some furniture that they didn't need anymore.

At that time, every newly-married couple got a credit from the state to make their start easier. It was a kind offering of seven thousand marks, worth about three thousand dollars, which enabled us to buy things like a bedroom set and a refrigerator. Dishwashers did not exist. For our wedding, my parents had given us a washing machine. Their support was incredible considering what they could afford. I also appreciated the efforts of my husband. He was not only getting our place ready but, at the same time, he was facing the beginning of his career as an army officer.

I was advised by my family to stay at their place until our new home was ready. I had already organized to give birth in the hospital in my parents' town. It was a modern place, provided with all the comfort one needed. I was not aware that the conditions might be different somewhere else. My desire to be together with my husband was getting stronger. I wanted to be by his side. I didn't want him to face everything alone over there so I took a decision. I decided to give birth to our child in the city in which we were going to live. My parents could understand my wish to be with my husband and it really seemed the right thing to do.

Hennigsdorf, 1988

After moving to Hennigsdorf and staying in the new place for five days with my husband, I went to the hospital. The doctor was very angry with me because I hadn't gone there on the first day of our arrival. I was very emotional about that. I hadn't meant to endanger my baby, as the doctor was suggesting. There was just so much happening at the same time. Anyway, regardless of whether the doctor was right or not, from that moment on, she had a prejudice against me.

The next evening my husband and I left for the hospital. Horst carried my suitcase and we walked for twenty minutes to the bus-station where we hoped to catch a bus or a taxi. It was raining and when we looked at the timetable, we saw that the next bus would only arrive in an hour's time. Had we waited for the bus, it would have meant that I was late for the time at which I had been ordered to the hospital. This was important to me and although it was pretty far away, we had no choice but to start on foot.

Naturally, we hoped that a car might stop and give us a lift. My husband was in a very bad mood, complaining that he would be back home late. I didn't mention that I was also feeling bad physically. I didn't want to make the situation worse than it already was. It was as if he had forgotten that I was nine months pregnant. After we had been slogging down the road for half an hour, a car finally stopped to pick us up and dropped us at the hospital.

My husband accompanied me inside and then went home. I didn't quite understand what his rush was for. Actually I had been hoping that we would have some time together since we had made it to the hospital before the appointed hour. I needed to talk a little about the extraordinary event which was to come. I wanted some company and emotional support in a matter which I felt was not entirely my own business.

As I sat there alone with my suitcase, waiting to be admitted, I felt as if I had been deserted. I was scared and began to cry. In the beginning, Horst had wanted to join me for the birth but his mother had told him that it was too disgusting to look at. I had looked forward to giving birth in a loving atmosphere but it was turning into something like the opposite. It would have been enough for me to know that he was around, somewhere near. Now I had to fight against the feelings of loneliness and shame that began to surround me. It made me feel as though giving birth was somehow unclean. I did not want to believe that and I was tired of seeing how Horst's mother could affect his life and how she was also, once again, affecting mine.

Eventually I was called into the Admissions Office where a nurse opened a file for me. This took about half an hour, during which time I was asked a lot of questions about the medical history of my family. The office was right beside the birthing-room and I could hear a woman screaming the whole time. The doctor, who was also the one who had ordered me to the hospital, came out and said to the nurse:

"It's a typical case of having a second baby. She knows what's coming . . ." I was highly intimidated and needed to gather all of my courage together, not to start yelling myself. I felt helpless. Slowly I saw my beautiful dream of having a baby falling apart.

In the days that followed, I felt terribly lonely. I wanted to be close to my husband but now he had no time to visit me. Once again, my expectations had given way to disappointment. I was afraid of losing my innocence in a different way. I felt exposed and vulnerable and treated as if I was just an object. The rude examinations were just one part, the other was the dirty conditions in the hospital.

It would have helped me to accept the circumstances more readily, had Horst been there to comfort me. At least I had my diary with me and I wrote down all the things I needed to express in order to be clear about what was happening. I really regretted not having stayed in my parents' town, where I could have been sure that my mother would have been around. The hospital was a disgrace compared to the neat institution in Frankfurt (Oder).

The place I was in was neither clean nor comfortable. The floors were dirty and the toilets down the hall were in no shape for sitting on. There were three toilets for the whole station and in one corner there was a one meter high paper bag with very smelly contents. There were no showers, nor could we take a bath. The only thing we had in our rooms was a stained sink. A woman could not feel very respected, being exposed to that kind of discomfort. It seemed to me that, because of our very special physical condition, we actually needed an ultra-clean environment.

Although it would probably have been possible, it did not cross my mind to change hospitals. Such a way of thinking was not common in our society. Apart from that, I was just about in shock at what was happening to me and it was too close to the birth for me to risk leaving.

The doctor thought I was late for confinement but said that she would wait five more days before inducing the baby's birth. After birth, it was the custom to stay in hospital for seven days so that meant I was going to spend almost two further weeks in that mess. Even though I felt discouraged by the news, I was able to pull myself together. I realized that I had to be strong for both my baby and myself. So I determined to make the best out of the situation. Beside my diary I had also brought a book of Russian with which I wanted to refresh my memory. I tried to keep myself busy as best I could, in order to avoid meditating too much about my surroundings.

When Horst came, he spent most of the time talking about the problems he was having fixing the apartment. I wanted to be an understanding wife and told myself that my problems were less important than his. After all, nothing around me confirmed that it could be very important to give birth. I couldn't wait to get back to normal life and be an active part of things but I had to finish my mission there and learn to have more patience. I was all the more happy when I heard that the next day, the doctor would induce the birth. I remembered all the things that I had learned in the preparatory course and while dreaming about being a mother soon, I thought of Horst. I was repressing the voice that wanted to tell me how much I felt rejected by his priorities. It would have hurt me too much and so I tried to convince myself of his good qualities. I liked the way he had started off in his job. His calm attitude calmed me too. I believed that he would be this way in everything he did and considered it to be a good trait. Today I know I misinterpreted his behavior. I only saw what I wanted to see.

In reality Horst was very often in the moon, far away from what was going on in front of him. I guess it was a kind of protection but at the same time, it was as if he was waiting for something. He seemed to be keeping silent, as if he didn't want to miss the sound of what he was searching for. Still he couldn't find it. It was probably long gone, along with deserted mother-love.

It was not yet time for me to stop kidding myself about how Horst really was. I drew a picture of him that helped me in the process I was then in. I imagined his strength. I imagined him as someone to lean on. I knew he had a hard time giving. I was afraid he might forget to bring flowers to the hospital after the birth. That would have been like him. I was afraid of the embarrassment in front of the other women in the room. In private it was different, even though I was hurt sometimes when I did not receive a gift for my birthday or at Christmas. I was at least able to keep quiet about it. I wanted to protect him. I thought that with love and time he would learn to be attentive. I tried to wash away the hurt and pictured us as a nice little family, with me being a good mom for our child and a reliable support for my husband in daily life.

I injected myself with optimism and tried to replace my worries about becoming a regular housewife with great happiness about doing so. I swore to myself that I was going to do all the necessary things without forgetting my own wishes. I had faith in our love and my own power of handling life.

The day of confinement came. I had the rare privilege of taking a bath in the morning and went into the birthing-room at eight o'clock. After six hours I gave birth to my wonderful baby boy, Jan. Horst called and was told to come and visit in two hours. When I woke up, the nurse offered to let me sit in a wheelchair. I was shy about Horst seeing me like that and tried to walk instead. Yet my legs didn't want to carry me and I was obliged to sit down in the wheelchair and let the nurse roll me down the hall-way to my room. Horst was already waiting there and to my embarrassment, he called me a grand-ma. It was his idea of a joke.

My parents and sister also came. My mother could not believe that I had given birth because I looked so relaxed. The next evening, both my husband and my father came again to bring more flowers which was very sweet of them. My father went back to Frankfurt (Oder) and during the following days and nights I was in a good deal of pain. Again Horst could not make it in to visit me. I had felt some kind of protection as long as my parents were around. Now when they were gone, Horst was gone as well. I thought the hurt of being left alone was going to burst me.

I was so inexperienced regarding babies that I could

not easily interpret the sounds Jan would make. Every time he cried it made me nervous and I had a hard time getting organized. The nurses didn't spend too much time in explanation and since I was alone in the room at that time, I had noone to help me or to talk to. At first I had problems breast-feeding and was distressed to see little Jan unable to drink. Naturally, he refused the bottle. I cried my eyes out, doubting if I was ever going to be able to give him what he needed. I was exhausted and had hardly energy left for myself.

Over the next few days things started to get much better and I began to follow up on a gymnastic program that had been suggested to me. I was feeling quite low emotionally and I thought that to be in good physical shape would counterbalance things. I spent long hours just looking at the baby, being truly happy for the first time since it had all begun. I sat, curiously watching his face and was satisfied to see him sleeping well. I felt secure then because I didn't really know what to do with him when he was awake. We were not allowed to take the babies into our beds because of the danger of bacterial infection. As well, I had gotten some infection of my own and when the doctor didn't want to send me home because of that, I had the guts to say:

"My infection probably came from the dirty toilets and it wouldn't help me to stay here anyway." Fortunately, the doctor agreed with me and I was released the next day.

Horst came to pick us up and our little family headed home. What a great moment! Arriving in the apartment, I was relieved to see how friendly this place looked compared to when I left. His efforts renewed my confidence that we would be able to build a happy future together. After staying home together for a few days, Horst went back to work and I was now to spend the next year at home with my baby son. That was a great thing for young families in our country. It meant we were able to stay at home during the first year of our baby's life, whilst still getting paid by our employer. As well, we had the guarantee that our job would be there after the baby year was over. That was the way our system worked. Social security was the main goal of society in spite of the fact that it was not always to the advantage of the economy.

It was wonderful to go for walks with Jan. The feeling of having gone through the birth and being slim again was great. I had a rush of wearing miniskirts and high heels after carrying a big belly for so long. I was not a great cook and actually forgot to eat when I was alone. I took care of my baby and did things around the house and lost even more weight.

One night Horst and I were invited to a party and I was not able to eat, my stomach not being used to a normal portion of food anymore. From then on I started to take better care of myself. At home I mostly listened to the radio. It was my partner during the day because I had noone to talk to. I didn't know my neighbors and nobody in the block was really friends with anybody else. The only connection between us all was that the men worked at the same place. They were all army people, just as the people living in my parents' block were all Security folk.

I went for regular check-ups with Jan and he was doing great. Sometimes when Horst worked at night and the baby cried I felt pretty helpless. Everything was still quite new for me and I could not always figure out what to do. One night Horst came home and found the two of us lying together on the bed and I was crying as loudly as the baby. I was at a point where I felt I couldn't deal with the baby all by myself, all the time. . Living in a strange town and not having my parents around, made me feel isolated from the rest of the world. My husband did not know what to do any more than I did and in the end, I simply had to go through the difficulties of the beginning by myself.

Every Friday, I had something that I looked forward to. I went back to Frankfurt (Oder) to take singing lessons with the teacher whose company and support I appreciated so much. She believed strongly in my artistic ability and encouraged me to keep going. Since my husband was working, Jan and I took the train over there together. It was our weekly outing and it was what kept me going through the rest of the week. The baby slept most of the time. Every once in a while, he would wake and drink from his bottle and then fall back into a satisfied sleep. In general, he was a very cooperative and friendly baby, sleeping well and smiling a lot.

Even though I was staying at home, I needed to keep in contact with the world. I was afraid of getting stuck in a domestic routine. Of course part of my obligations were domestic but I needed to have more than that. The music never let me go. So I always kept my eye open for a chance to develop my artistic abilities. Even though it was not an easy task to travel with my baby every week it was healthy for my state of mind. I needed the feeling of accomplishment. My son was my treasure and I sheltered him with love and strength. When we came along people used to be very sympathetic and I never needed to ask for help carrying the stroller upstairs or down, or out of the train or into it. There was always somebody right beside us to lend a hand.

My parents used to wonder where I took the energy from to go back and forth like that. Motivation was the real key to it. Horst also supported my idea of getting into music seriously and encouraged me to stick to my plan. However, there was another reason why I returned to my parents' city each week. I was not happy in my new town nor was my couple life working out anywhere near how I had imagined it. It was so boring all day and at night, I could not manage to get my husband to talk. It wasn't easy for him because he came home exhausted from work to find me desperately waiting to have someone to talk to. I have to admit that we were not able to create a homely atmosphere. We did not feel very inspired by each other and somehow we just came to accept our circumstances and the dark and humid apartment that went with them.

One morning after Horst had left for work, I went to make the bed and spotted a silver fish on the pillow. I wasn't absolutely sure whether or not it was vermin but when I moved the pillow it scuttled off. I was stunned by this discovery. I hated things which crawled.

Later I talked to one of my neighbors about it and she told me that she woke up one morning with just such a thing perched on her eyelid. That was a horror story for me and that evening I had to beg Horst to lift the mattress with me, in order to see if there were any more. Underneath we found a nightmare. There were whole congregations of these worms under our bed.

Living directly over the basement and the apartment being very humid, it was a terrific place for them to multiply. Although we cleaned up, they always came back. I think we used to bring some of them up from the cellar every time we went to fetch coal. An exterminator couldn't do much because of the building itself. It had been built in the wintertime and it had lots of holes and cracks in the floors and walls. It would have needed major reconstruction in order to do anything about it.

So instead of getting better, the problem got worse and we had regular fights against spiders and ants which made it impossible to feel comfortable in that place. My husband didn't really mind but I felt unable to sleep in that bed any longer. Overnight I stayed on the couch where I felt a bit safer. Of course that created problems for us as a couple and my husband got mad about me being so sensitive.

After we had been there only a few weeks, Horst and I got into an argument. I was busy cleaning the dishes and he wanted to know why I was doing it in the evening when I supposedly had all day to do it. He used to drink quite a bit and that evening, before I really knew what was happening, I found myself on the floor with a bloody nose and a broken tooth. I was unable to move, my head was spinning and I saw stars all around me.

My husband was terrified at what he had done and carried me to the bed. For my part, I was sorry that I had made him so angry and was not really aware at the time, that nothing could have justified such behavior. That was the evening before we were supposed to pick up my piano. The next day my nose was like a blue-green potato and I had to explain to people that a curtain pole had fallen on my face. I repeated the same story to my family until Horst told his own parents the truth. He was probably afraid of himself. In a way, he was calling for help.

I was mad that the whole thing had come out for I felt embarrassed that our parents might think I had failed in my marriage. Finally, it was I who ended up feeling responsible for that violent act. I said to myself, if I had been a different person, he wouldn't have done it. My son was sleeping at the time of the incident, so fortunately he didn't come into it. I felt my life was taking a strange course. First I had to live through the pain of bearing a child and then, at a time when I was still not feeling normal again, I had to experience the pain of being beaten.

I could not begin to understand where life was leading me. The feeling of humiliation made me very angry and I started to be fed up with my circumstances. Still, I was not yet frustrated enough to undertake the necessary changes. By refusing to act, I accepted the continuing atmosphere of depression and this in spite of my deteriorating emotional health. I concentrated on taking care of my baby and kept on going on Fridays to the music school. The used piano that we had was old and smelly. I was so desperate to do music that I didn't care about its pitiful state when I got it. However, since it was incapable of being tuned, I finally had to put it in the garbage. So much for music in that house.

Winter came and it was incredibly difficult to warm the place. My husband and I were often arguing and going to bed angry. I could not endure finishing so many evenings like that and cried for hours until I fell asleep exhausted. I was so terribly sad to see my romantic ideas of marriage drowning in icy water. Horst used to say that it was me who couldn't deal with myself. I suppose that was true to an extent but he didn't really know how to handle his own emotions, either. Of course there were also positive moments. We loved to go to the restaurant or the cinema and we sometimes went dancing.

We were a couple who had thought we were made for one another. We had believed that we needed each other and that we therefore had to make it work, no matter what. Our child played an important role, since both Horst and I valued our roles as Papa and Mama. Also, we wanted to prove to our parents that we could manage our life together. We were so optimistic in the beginning believing that we could move mountains with our love. Now I find myself wondering whether our love was too small or the mountain too big.

In the spring of 1989, on my way back from a trip to my parents, I was nearing home when a neighbor crossed my path. She asked me if I had heard what had happened. I had no idea what she could be talking about. Finally she told me what she had herself seen. In the early morning a noise had woken up the whole house. Apparently it was caused by soldiers banging on the door of our apartment. They were trying to get in and finally they jumped onto the balcony and got in that way. The person they had been looking for was my husband. What had happened?

I rushed home, pushing the baby carriage as fast as I could. There I found a paper on the kitchen table. It was from Horst, a short note written in his small handwriting:

Something bad has happened to me, please stay by my side, Pina. I need you now, I love you.

I still had no idea of what was going on. I took my baby and went to buy some groceries. As I walked along in front of the apartment block, people looked at me in a way that made me worry even more. Some were staring at me with pity in their eyes. Still others looked at me with contempt, or so I imagined. When I came back, two neighbors were standing in the hall, talking about Horst. They finally told me that he had beaten up five people in a restaurant. It was following a party with some of his soldier friends. I could not believe what I was hearing.

As much as I wanted to distance myself from the abominable act, I was dying to hear the truth from his own lips. I still lived in the hope that it was a mistake of some kind until he finally arrived home and confirmed that everything was true. I could not understand what was happening with him. He said that some of the soldiers had refused to pay the bill and left it up to him and he had therefore found it appropriate to knock them down. In the skirmish, he had decided to include a civilian who had had nothing to do with the whole thing.

The following weeks were filled with a lot of trouble. Therapy was an unknown word in our society. Not that help didn't exist but somehow the idea of counselling was connected with the treatment of mentally ill people. Everything was supposed to be solved by a person being called to account and by the use of disciplinary measures. Instead of people being helped to change, they were intimidated and developed yet more frustration for the next time they would blow up. The only thing that was done to Horst was that he was placed in a military hospital for two weeks. There he was examined for psychiatric abnormalities. During that time he kept on telling me how much it meant to him that I was standing by his side and how everybody else was an idiot except for me. Everybody deserves a second chance and I would have felt pretty bad to leave him. It was natural for me as his wife to fight it through with him, even though my reputation had been damaged as well, by his behavior.

The shockwaves from this incident were calming down slowly when Horst came home one day with a serious expression on his face. Standing in the living room, he said that he had heard something bad about me from his mother. My heart wanted to stop and a heatwave went through my body. I had the worst feeling about what was to come as I asked him what it was this time that his mother might have to say about me. She had told him that I had been called in front of a commission and was being obliged to give an account of my intention not to go back to work. My own reasoning for this had apparently been that my husband would make enough money for both of us. This was, furthermore, the reason I had not been accepted into the Communist Party.

I almost fainted when I heard that. First of all, the story as he had been told, was untrue. Secondly, I could not understand where the material for the story might have come from. I cried and said that I could no longer accept a relationship where such false accusations destroyed his trust in me over and over again.

After desperately trying to remember what this story

could be based on, I thought back to two years earlier when I was looking for a way to study music after college. That's when I had been to City Hall to consult a woman about the possibility of staying home after college. I had known that it was even less appropriate to admit that I wanted to study music instead. Her aggressive reaction had given me the shivers and I had felt a good deal of active dislike coming from her.

That woman had obviously known who I was because she was, as Horst later told me, an acquaintance of his mother. He was torn apart between the two very different stories and did not know whom to believe. He finally came to the conclusion that his mother could have no reason to make up a story like that. His mother had also told him it was understandable that he had become violent with a woman like me at his side. Too often I saw him look at me with doubtful eyes, heard him judge me with a reproachful voice, felt him treat me like some kind of suspect. It was more than I was willing to take. I was disgusted to see that, whilst I had stood by his side when he had had to face charges, his family were willing to turn things around to make me look bad and put me on trial as well. I felt I was ready for divorce.

Horst wasn't sure if I was serious but when I showed him the papers he got anxious and asked for some outside help to keep us together. One evening we had a visitor who introduced himself as a member of the Secret Service. We talked about the situation in our marriage, about Horst's criminal act and about the never-ending accusations of his mother against me. I was reminded that I was married to an officer and that in the context, it was definitely appropriate to be strong and to stay on with him. I replied that I also needed him to be strong for me. In fact, my request for a divorce wasn't due to not loving him any more, it was because of the degrading circumstances which surrounded us and which I was unable to change. By Horst saying that he would, from then on, stand by my side, I decided to change my mind. The guy from Security finally advised me to destroy the divorce papers and I decided to do so. For the moment, that was an end to it.

One day, while driving with my parents in their car, I saw an advertisement in a newspaper from a radio station. It was asking people to send in sample demos of their songs for an amateur contest. When I read this my heart went on fire. Sitting in the back of the car I tried not to make any noise while I tore the advertisement from the page and then hid it secretly in my pocket. My mother turned around to ask me what I was doing but I managed to keep it secret. I knew all too well that she would just tell me once again to stop dreaming. I had no interest in that kind of advice. I was determined to go and find that dream and to make it a reality.

With much enthusiasm, I set out to prepare a demo on a little tape-recording machine I owned. I wanted to present my own melodies accompanied by my guitar. Before I started to play, I said on the cassette that I would first give a version of an international hit by the Bangles so that the jury could have a chance to get used to my voice. I gave them a rendition of 'Eternal flame', a popular tune of that time. Then I presented a couple of my own compositions. As I mailed the package, I was pretty nervous but I said to myself that I had nothing to lose. I felt like somebody dropping a bottle with a letter in the ocean, hoping for someone to recognize a sign of life inside. Nevertheless, I had some confidence that I would be discovered.

It was August then and in October I was going to work in school. For now, I was still home with my boy, in the baby year.

Hungary, 1989

I remember a conversation between my husband and I in July 1989 during which we expressed our joint opinion that we could not live in a better country. For us that was the perfect land. There were no earthquakes, no wars, no poverty, no fight for survival, everything was there. We had work, apartments, social security, special support for families. We had no idea that the socialist system was about to break down.

I don't know how long the system might have continued on its way, had not socialist Hungary opened up its borders to capitalist Austria. Hungary was a popular place for vacations for East German people. Since people didn't have the chance to travel wherever they wanted to, Hungary, which had a certain western flavor and was less tough in its thinking, was a welcome getaway.

When the borders to Austria were opened during the high summer season of 1989, large numbers of people from the GDR grabbed the chance to take off for the West. Most of them were star-gazing about thoughts of freedom and many did not even stop to consider that they were leaving their homes and in some cases, their families, behind them. People left in a hurry, afraid that the border might close again at any moment. The whirlpool of enthusiasm, the sudden chance to break out and the dizziness brought on by such a drastic change, caused a sort of electricity to flow through the holidaymakers. Vistas of new opportunities seemed suddenly to be opening up. A whole population was being infused with a new energy.

So peoples' main goal was first to get out, then they could think of everything else. Most of the fleeing East Germans planned to reach West Germany. Crossing the border from Hungary into Austria gave them the status of political refugees. Within a few days, hundreds of emergency shelters for thousands of fleeing people were built. Families, young couples, singles, groups of friends, almost everyone who happened to be on vacation when Hungary opened the border, headed towards the West. This sudden determination left no space for questions or doubts. The power of the people was so immense, it was a shock to themselves and the whole world.

When the news hit it was like a coming out. As I watched the television with my husband, my mouth stood open, then my heart started pounding and within seconds I saw a stream of confused images passing in front of my eyes. It was as if my body was going through some kind of potentially terminal shock. There I sat with my concept of life firmly anchored in what I had for so long been taught. I acknowledged the news with disbelief and was simply amazed at the number of citizens who were leaving the country in such a hurry. I wasn't sure whether to applaud or to blame them. I thought that the borders were probably going to be closed very soon and then everything would return to normal.

Over the next few weeks, people kept on rushing to Austria and I began to experience a loss of orientation. The thought of leaving the country didn't cross my mind at that time. The official East German news broadcasts were still being blown up with the usual success-oriented reports of socialist production. It was also reported that the number of people who had left was insignificant compared to the number of East Germans who would stand behind their country. It was called a period of limited rebellion, a result of the Cold War that had blinded some of 'our' people.

They also informed us about demonstrations of civilians. A wave of new thinking was gathering force. The old regime was not acceptable anymore. The limitations it had imposed on peoples' lives had brought their frustration to a peak. I was amazed to think how the system had kept functioning if so many people had been fed up with it for so long. The authorities decided not to fight the movement with the army or by means of violence. Besides, the number of demonstrators was so large that any violent acts of repression would have been but a bloody confirmation of the wrongness of the regime.

I have learned that the knowledge I got from news broadcasts was not always true. Still, the general position of the regime was a mild one, even though it kept on trying to convince people to stay with them. This process of change was called the 'peaceful revolution'. When I saw extracts of demonstrations on TV, I heard the spokespersons say not to let go of the peaceful revolution, to stay determined but not to undertake any violent actions. People respected the regime for not using the power of the army to counter the movement. Some of the senior people in the system tried to use persuasion on people, trying to warn them about throwing away everything too hastily. However, the anger of the people was too great, there was no room for 'one more try'. It was finished for too many. The trust was gone.

The time from August to November 1989 flew away like nothing. The weeks were filled with daily demonstrations, a never-ending stream of people leaving for 'holidays' in Hungary. Meanwhile the government was still trying to save the sinking ship by appealing to the people not to forsake their society.

In the late evening of November 9th, more wall-breaking news hit the people. A spokesperson for the government relayed the reports of the long hoped-for but hitherto unexpected event, that from now on the borders between East and West Germany were open. We were free to go. The news caused mixed feelings amongst those who had so far stayed put. What did it all mean? Was there only one Germany now?

Right after that, a stream of cars, especially the East's famous Trabants, with the awful clouds of smoke coming out of their tailpipes, moved towards West Berlin. Suddenly the city, which had been split in two for twenty eight years, was experiencing a reunion of Germans. People were greeted with champagne and flowers were piled on top of their cars as they moved forward. It was like a parade and the atmosphere was that of a carnival. In the first days, there was a sense of overwhelming happiness. There was such emotion in people's voices when, afterwards, they recounted the experience of visiting the West for the first time. It is difficult to imagine the extent of that feeling of joy mixed with wonder, which flowed throughout the East in those early days of reunification.

My disappointment in the system and the embarrassment I felt towards people that used to tell me that I was a blind believer in it, made me dizzy. Although I kept watching the news broadcasts, I was seeing them in a completely different light. I realized the huge span of truth between the language they used and the reality on the streets. All the kids at school had teased me for wearing 'pink glasses'. Now I could understand what they had been getting at and I was angry about them myself.

I expelled a system from my heart that had so obviously abandoned me a long time ago, by abusing my trust. There was still little effort being made to pay the respect to the people which they deserved: by telling the truth. I had been fooled like thousands of others and I was determined to make the best out of the new situation. I told myself I would never again serve a society before taking care of my own needs. That meant the beginning of a voyage along a road which I would find by following my own beliefs.

While hitchhiking I was picked up by a lot of people who told me what they were thinking. I got a picture of many different points of view but everybody was uncertain about what would happen next. On the outside I still used the language of socialism. I was insecure, as I imagine were many others. Nobody knew how things might turn out and nobody was willing to predict which way things would fall.

Shortly after this I found myself being magically transported into the dream world of that other city behind the wall.

West Berlin, November 1989

The bus slowly went its way along the street. It was dark. I watched out the window, still trying to bring some order to my thoughts. The wall around the western part of Berlin had no meaning anymore, except that it was now an historic monument. Beside me in the bus sat my husband and a friend of ours. They were joking and having a good time. We were on the way to Berlin; West Berlin.

That particular Saturday the three of us had been sitting in a cafe in the afternoon when one of the guys suddenly said: why don't we go for a ride to West Berlin? Our city was only twenty minutes distance from the West but in order to reach East Berlin, the train had previously been obliged to go all around the border of the Western part and it had taken more than one hour to get there. After the wall had come down it took much less time to enter the city because we could travel right through the centre. I needed to take a deep breath because even the suggestion of going to the West turned something in my stomach around. At this point many of the former believers were still suffering from shock at the surprise of it all and it caused them and it caused them disbelief rather than relief.

Although I agreed to go with them I wasn't really sure if technically, it would be legal. Could we really just cross to the West? Horst and his friend both worked as officers for the East German border patrol. I was working in school and still educating kids in a socialist context. What's more, I was the daughter of parents who worked for the Secret Service. I could not get it straight in my mind as to whether or not we were setting a bad example as leaders. As much as I was curious to know what was on the other side, I was afraid to make a mistake. I asked the guys what *they*, our parents, our bosses and the Party, were going to think about us. What would my parents say if they knew I had been to see the West, when they were still criticizing my grandmother for watching western channels. And what about the people who I was sure were watching us to see how we, the representatives of socialism, would act or behave.

O.k. so there was no socialist power anymore to blame us but what about our ideals? I thought of calling my parents. They should know what was the right thing to do and be able to say what was really going on. They always knew. Yet I still wasn't sure if it was a trick concocted by our government to prove who was true to the system and who was going to use the first opportunity to get out. Anyway, I decided to take a chance because it looked like the news had to be real.

Sitting in the bus, I felt my East German passport so clearly in my pocket, like a mark of where I came from and where I belonged. As we approached the border, I prepared myself for different possibilities. I wondered whether the East might arrest us for betraying our country or whether the West would send us right away to a concentration camp when they found out who we were. That's what my father had always told me they would do. Even if everything should go well, I expected at the least, to have a bunch of questions put to me.

When we arrived we had to leave the bus to enter a building to pass the control. I was busy thinking about the right answers to possible questions. Standing in front of the East German officer, he looked at the picture in my passport, then looked at me and said with a smile, o.k. We got back in the bus and entered West Berlin, the territory of the former enemy.

I couldn't believe it was happening. For all the twenty years of my life, I had never considered this kind of situation for a moment. The wall in Berlin was as natural to me as day following night. I never would have guessed that it would ever change. Now I wasn't even asked a single question! Nobody seemed to care where I was going or why. The border guards smiled in a relaxed fashion as if, in the past, they had never looked at people with bull-dog faces. Instead, they seemed as if they had been used to this situation all their lives. I found out later that the army, including the customs officers, had been ordered to be cooperative and not to show any signs of antipathy.

Upon entering the streets of West Berlin, I wondered if people would recognize us as the Eastern birds we were, because of our clothes and appearance. Women from the East did not leave a cloud of strong perfume behind them or put their chin up while walking down the street. My husband and his friend regained their relaxed attitude and we were soon busy taking in the sea of commercial lights on the building fronts. Because of all the colors it was much brighter than anything we were used to.

At first I was a bit intimidated, watching all those secure, strong-willed looking people. Later I realized that this was a way they had, of protecting themselves against any kind of importunity. The more secure someone looked, the smaller the chances were that he would be bothered. What surprised me most was that the streets were so clean and the windows full of such beautiful things. I could not see a trace of dirt or of the poverty and crime which had been part of my picture of the West.

I was told that it was all kept hidden under the glamour of Western wealth. When I saw my parents after I had been to the West for the first time, I told them about the wonderful things I had seen. I was almost proud to inform them about how clean the city looked. I think I wanted partly to make them feel better about the change because they were looking at the future with very negative expectations. And yes, in the following weeks I did see people sitting on the side of the street, looking pitiful, begging for something and I did see musicians who were trying to earn some money by performing on the street. Their faces were sometimes melancholic, sometimes empty.

The strange thing was that they were sitting on the same streets that I had walked down at first yet I had not seen them then. I had probably been so busy watching all those lights that I forgot to look down. After having discovered the other side of the coin, I was frightened by these scenes. We were not used to anything like that. There was a strange sense of a perilous condition of life hanging over the West and it's not something I am comfortable with, even today.

In the beginning I always gave something to a person who I saw was in desperate need. Once I gave the sandwich that I had just started to eat, to a hungry girl who was begging. Another time in a store, an old woman wanted to buy a loaf of bread but was short of money. Her face showed so much despair that I could not let her walk away without the bread and I paid for her. Her astonishment and happiness showed me that these acts of support might be rare because people had gotten used to seeing other people in need. And it is true that by giving a little money we don't change anything in the long run. I started to recognize that many people had faces like masks. There was something stiff and lifeless about their expressions. Some of the women wore so much makeup as if they were trying to hide their vulnerability beneath it.

Germans are especially known for their borderless enthusiasm, when they believe in something. That goes for the good as well as for the bad energies. So far so good. The waking up to reality was not too long in coming. We found that, after the initial headiness of parties in the streets, things were not as rosy as they looked. The Trabants were no longer welcome in the West, because of their damage to the environment. The money in our savings books was divided in about two after the fusion of the two marks. There was a very limited acceptance of East German diplomas or work experience. There were factory closings, outright bankruptcies and widespread unemployment. These social emergencies, caused by the collapse of the old system, were just a portion of the hard reality that East Germans had to face after the first enthusiasm had waned.

There were two factors which caused much of the unnecessary personal tragedies which followed upon the dismantling of the wall. There was the fact that the government of the West had little interest in the structures of the former East. All kinds of souvenirs of the old regime, including buildings that recalled the East too much, were destroyed and replaced by something more in keeping with the spirit of the times. By the same token, many eastern people were also impatient to throw out the window everything that smelled of the vanished socialism. It seemed they just wanted to commit themselves totally to the new and glorious life that they thought was waiting for them. It did not take too long for a lot of that glory to melt to illusion. Many bright hopes were simply buried under the more urgent need to struggle to survive.

Yet noone can blame the Easterners for being naive. We were not educated to think for ourselves, to compare the good and bad sides. In the past we were supposed to take what we got and to believe what we were taught. We had also taken many things for granted which cost a lot of money in the West. Underlying all this was the basic teaching that our system was totally right and everything else wrong. Even though many ought to have known better, they had allowed themselves to be influenced by it because they lived in the middle of it.

Many people took part in the system in an automatic fashion, because there was no other choice. This fact was pivotal in the eventual undermining of the system itself. The only thing one could do was to develop some kind of protection. Like someone who has been forbidden to walk, even though he wants to very much, he still falls over when the day comes that he takes his first steps. The East German people had had too many such falls and had to learn to walk very slowly at first. Many of those who tried to run, tripped up badly.

After the first flush of enthusiasm about their new freedom, people had to face a very strange reality. To be able to buy all the nice things you needed money. An unknown number of men left their families to try their luck alone in the new world without spending one more thought or penny on those they left behind. West Germany now had the responsibility of keeping their newest citizens motivated and of introducing them into the context of capitalism.

Everybody, including children, received a welcome gift of one hundred Deutschmarks. At that time, there was an incredible amount of movement from East to West. Buses were overloaded and lines of a hundred or more meters were waiting for the next bus to leave for West Berlin. The shopping centers were overflowing and for a few weeks it looked as if the West had been taken over by the East. Especially the cosmetic shops and sex shops were filled with action-hungry eastern people.

At the same time you could see frustration on western peoples' faces. They now had to wait in line and accept that a lot of new brothers and sisters had come to share their kingdom. I had the feeling that we East Germans were considered as foreigners, even though we were now supposed to be one nation. It was not easy to unite two such different societies. It was natural that we were going to face a long period of adaptation. The enthusiasm was slowly fading and after the first rush of buying western products was finished, it didn't take long for many eastern people to start complaining again.

The one hundred Deutschmarks hadn't lasted too long and people were now facing the Union of Exchange. The East German currency was of no real value in the capitalist economy. The compromise was to turn it into West German money by cutting all the savings of East Germans in half. This was in fact a generous arrangement although there was a maximum that was allowed to be exchanged. Many people simply lost everything that exceeded that maximum rate. For several weeks there were line-ups of hundreds of people in front of every bank in the East, as people tried to find ways to keep as much of their savings as possible.

Since everything had happened so fast, the new economy did not really have a chance to get established, while the old one virtually stopped overnight. The unemployment rate shot up and our people had to get used to going to buildings to seek employment opportunities for the first time in their lives. This was an almost degrading place to be for people who had always had a job.

People adjusted quite fast to the look of western clothes, to makeup and perfumes. Soon it was hard to determine who came from which side. It was in the language that we could hear the difference. Although they came from the same city, people from the East side spoke the Berlin slang while people from the West spoke High German. Of course we knew how to speak it too but we preferred to use the bold slang of the streets.

The peaceful revolution was going to create some not so peaceful effects in peoples' lives. The East quickly became the black sheep of the nation and only over the years will it be possible for a complete adjustment to be made. That was partly the fault of the East Germans themselves because they gave up one kind of freedom too rapidly without considering what lay in front of them. Most of them saw only one side of the coin, as it was expressed in words like freedom, choice, fashion, beauty, cars, credit and so on. They forgot to consider the other side seriously enough before agreeing to such an extreme change. Now for the first time, they had to face competition, higher living costs, unemployment and a completely different approach to life, on top of the loss of all the social advantages they had been used to.

One thing that surprised me greatly was the reaction of certain people, including my husband and some of the other officers I knew. All ideals and former goals seemed to vanish at once. All the big words about their dedication to socialism disappeared on the winds of change. Diplomas, papers, even books and passports and all kinds of socialist paraphernalia landed in the garbage faster than the wall could be taken down. Even though I could share the anger about having been fooled for so long by the old society, I could not agree to flushing every part of my past so quickly. Some people knew right away what the new society was all about and made good money by selling original army clothes, buttons, medals and pieces of the wall.

All these events put a powerful brake on my own rising enthusiasm. I tried to keep some rationality going throughout all the changes. It was easy to feel a bit like Alice in Wonderland and go around with wide staring eyes. My education, which had not concentrated on consumer values, enabled me to stay alert while facing that new and overwhelming wealth. I kept my eyes open because it did not feel right to me to switch horses too fast. I started a process of seriously questioning everything I had experienced up until then, trying to take a closer look at the new society without the prejudices I had been taught.

My feeling that our behavior was going to be observed by others was soon confirmed. I confessed to a colleague of mine at school that I had been to West Berlin on the weekend. When I began to talk about the positive surprises I had had when I got there, she commented to someone else:

"That's typical, the strongest believers are now the first ones to be found in western shopping centers." I could understand her frustration, even though I had wanted her to understand that my picture of the West had been very wrong. I guess it was too late then to be accepted by those people who had hoped and waited for this change so desperately.

The sweeping changes going on included a very important personal change for me, one that I was not aware of right away. Many professional papers and diplomas were not accepted in the new system. It was simply not possible to transfer from one ideology to the other and so many people, regardless of whether they were young or old, had to go back to school and get themselves qualified all over again. The teaching profession was one in particular which was considered to need modification. So I suddenly found myself faced with the possibility of being unable to continue teaching. The loophole had come of its own accord!

Meanwhile, I had made a pretty decent contact in the

one and only radio station in East Berlin. I had rather vague hopes as to whether they would ever get back to me so I was all the more surprised when I received a letter from them one day. It contained a positive reaction to my demo tape. I had made it through the first stage of selection and was invited to the station where I gave my first radio interview. I was still busy digesting this unexpected success when they offered to produce a good quality demo in one of their studios. I was overwhelmed by the speed with which the door had been opened to me and I determined to keep my foot in it.

I started to receive letters and telegrams from the station with information about contacts and appointments. I could hardly believe that I had made it that far. I was still living in that dark, unpromising apartment but suddenly everything was becoming illuminated by the light of a new hope. I was being offered the chance to do what deep down I most desired to do. It was an incredible time.

I had to make phone-calls fairly often and since we did not have a phone of our own, I was obliged to walk twenty minutes down to the post office. I remember that the phone-booth was small and smelly and the windows would steam up after a short while. I used to get out of there sweating but immensely happy about my contacts to the world of showbiz. It was as if my optimism made me grow wings. There was so much that was positive at that time that I could even endure having to go to school each day.

By the middle of winter, the general mood in Germany was sinking. People were worried about their jobs and many were devastated to learn that they had to go back to school. For some it was as if their personal clocks had been put back decades. For some reason, a lot of new shopping-centers were built where the people could spend the money they didn't have. There were not enough jobs being created which caused an economic imbalance. Lots of products from the West were put in eastern stores but nobody could afford them. One after the other, the production of eastern products was suspended.

Since there was no work in the East, people started to look for jobs in the West and that caused more conflict. Eastern employees were always paid less than their western counterparts, no matter what their qualifications. Since they needed the money, many of them travelled as much as six hours daily by bus or car to go to work in the West. More and more Westerners watched angrily as East Germans went to work on the jobs which they believed should have belonged to them. One can imagine what kind of stress that caused between the so-called brothers and sisters of the new state.

That difficult situation also created fertile ground for the seeding of the neo-nazi movement which gave vent to people's frustration. Perhaps the main problem of all was that of adapting to the idea of competition. People were given the chance to learn useful skills within jobtraining programs organized by the government. Yet, notwithstanding the first cold shower that had paralyzed many, there still seemed to be an almost general lack of motivation on the part of the former socialists. People had nothing to hold on to and it seemed as though many of them were out of breath from the rapid changes which should have taken place over years, not months.

I did not share the pessimism that suddenly surrounded eastern people. It was as if my life had just begun. In January of 1990, I was offered a chance to sing two songs in the biggest cultural building of the East. It was at that time that I took the final decision to change my professional direction for good. After resigning, I stopped working at school at once. The legal system of the East did not work anymore anyway, while the one in the West hadn't made its way through yet. This allowed me to slip through the holes in the law and give my life a new direction. The loss of professional status which was ruining so many of my former countrymen gave me the biggest opportunity I'd ever had. Although my husband had by then ceased to work at the border, he was still employed, dismantling army stations. That meant we still had some sort of income to see us through the first period of reunification.

Meanwhile, I tried to be accepted at the Classical Music University in Berlin but that didn't work out. I wasn't discouraged by the refusal. I was hanging on to my dream even more strongly, saying to myself that I was probably not meant to become an opera singer. So I started to produce the two demo songs in the studio, as had been agreed with the radio station. The person who worked with me was a passionate musician himself and supported me very much. Together we won the amateur contest and the winner's prize was to make a real production of the songs in the biggest studio in Berlin.

Western companies were getting more and more involved in the development of the market in the East. The radio station I was connected with was itself taken over. I was subsequently invited to the station in order to meet members of a record company who were searching for new talent. They had listened to several artists from our side and wanted to choose three, with whom they said they were willing to produce an album.

When I received this invitation I really had to sit down. I could not believe that I was one of the ones being selected, when there were so many other established and talented artists. Horst shared in my happiness and believed more and more that it would be worthwhile for me to stick to the music business. By that stage, my parents were ready for almost any surprise and they encouraged me to make my way too. Like so many other things around us, their interest in seeing me continue as a teacher had waned considerably. It was just not the same anymore in the light of the capitalist society.

I went to the appointment with a great deal of curiosity. The boss of the radio station expressed enthusiasm about my chances and tried to be positive with me. Still, I could sense his nervousness. Nobody's job was safe at that time. There was a weird race going on everywhere as to who was going to make it through and who would have to go out and start again somewhere else. This was going on just below the surface. It didn't have much effect on me at the time although it set the tone for what is often a fickle industry.

When the two western producers entered the room, they had their sunglasses on and smelt strongly of cologne. They were both loud and exuberant and made me a little ill at ease. Since I couldn't see their eyes, I wondered whether I should look at their noses or the frames of their dark glasses as I stood up to greet them. We soon began an interesting conversation, however and I was astonished by their determination to work with me. It seemed as though I had truly entered another world.

A few weeks later I got my artist's contract and had my first appearance on TV. People were amazed to hear about the unusual progress I had made. It seemed to them that I had come out of nowhere. Here I was, without any warning, one of the first to have a record contract with the West. Was I ever motivated about that!

In the first weeks, we worked in the studio in East Berlin and then we finished the production in the Berlin Hansa Studio over on the western side. I was quite an inexperienced singer at that time, particularly with regard to studio work. Most of the songs and lyrics had been written for me and at times I did not even know what I was singing about. I had problems overcoming the shyness I felt at performing in front of a studio crew. Nor had I yet completely developed my singing technique. Sometimes I felt discouraged because I wasn't sure if my dream of being a singer was really meant to be.

Of my two producers, one was of a tough nature and told me, very shortly, just to spit it out. The other was more understanding. He constantly encouraged me by saying that I was getting better. He also spent time talking with me about different techniques, such as ways to make emotions show up in my voice. The musical direction of the album was pop-rock and I had a chance to learn to give everything my voice could give at that time.

For the first time ever, I was invited to Italian restaurants and learned how to eat spaghetti. It was a period filled with novelty. When my husband had the time he joined me in the studio and got to know the musicians and producers. He seemed to like it all and kept on supporting me. Since it was taking a lot of time to travel back and forth from home, it was suggested that I stay for one week with a family living near the studio. After discussing it with Horst, he agreed to take care of Jan. They both came to visit me that week and we spent an afternoon in the studio together. From what he said, everything was fine between us.

When I came home, a neighbor told me that Horst talked to others about what we would buy with the money when I would be a star. At the same time, he had expressed his fears that I might not stand by his side once I reached the top, in spite of all he had done for me. All the big talk about stars and dreams and fears stunned me somehow. It sounded naive to me but I understand now that this was only my point of view. It was not my style to make a noise about something that wasn't even reality. All I wanted was to work my way up in a fair way, taking one step at a time. I must admit that I liked to act secretly and didn't want too much attention on me while I was trying something new. Probably that came from fear of failure.

I grew more and more displeased to hear that my husband was making a big fuss about everything. He was putting me on a pedestal on the one hand and letting me down on the other with his lack of trust. When I questioned him about it, he said that he was not sure that I was being true to him. I had heard that story from him before and I wasn't more prepared to accept it then. I thought that only faith and honesty could allow us to make it through all the changes and new developments in our lives.

The situation between us did not improve afterwards. Besides our generally strained relationship, Horst could not stop watching action movies on the new video-recorder we had bought. In our old society, such things had not even existed and a video-recorder was the first thing many East Germans bought. Horst was in charge of our finances and one day he told me that we had nothing left but twenty Deutschmarks. I said that I would get another job that would help us make it through.

The thing that upset me very much was that Horst took the twenty marks and spent it on video cassettes for the recording of action movies instead of buying food that we urgently needed. My request that he spend our last few coins on groceries, fell on deaf ears. It worried me considerably to see that there might be something more important to him than making sure his family had food on the table.

The next day I left early in the morning for West Berlin. I had seen an advertisement in the paper for a hospital which was looking for people to do the cleaning. Since I was not familiar with the western side of the city, it took me a few hours to get to my destination. I was accepted and after the paper work in the administration building was done, I headed right away to the hospital to start working. By telling them it was an emergency, I managed to get an advance on my pay after my first day of work. I went home exhausted but happy to have two hundred good marks in my pocket.

I got home around midnight. Horst was there and he invited me to watch a horror film with him. Yet again he surprised me by not asking any questions about my day, nor showing any signs of appreciation about my contribution to the family treasury. Anyway, I sat down to spend the rest of the evening with him. Due to my physical exhaustion and the stress of the last weeks, I was not quite able to digest a horror film in which a child, who had been run over by a truck, came back from the grave as a monster that killed everybody in sight.

I didn't think of the possibility that Horst might have been frustrated about my progress, since he knew he was soon to face unemployment. When he suddenly shouted at me that I should leave the room if I was too sensitive to look at such a film, I started crying. The evening was over. Horst was angry and I was emotionally at the end of my tether. I spent half the night in tears while Horst slept. This kind of situation was no longer new to me and I felt that I was going to destroy myself if I kept on living in these circumstances.

My frustration had reached its peak and suddenly I saw very clearly what I had to do. I needed to free myself from a pattern of life which wasn't doing me any good. No matter who was right or wrong, I realized that I was not able to change it for the better. This last experience, though not extreme in itself, had been the drop which overflowed a cup already too full of crazy emotions. Over the previous months, I had seen that my husband had lost more and more of his concern regarding his family.

Besides the general loss of direction, there was one thing in particular I couldn't stand. The hurtful reproach from Horst that I would leave him after I had become successful, lived with me at all times like a bad spirit. I was finally disheartened enough to draw the line. I was so angry to be mistrusted that I decided to continue on my artistic path without a husband who, while taking all the credit, gave me only prejudices to live on.

That night, I urged myself to stop finding excuses for the conditions in my life and do something about it. I immediately stopped crying when I was clear about my decision. The feeling of being imprisoned was all of a sudden, gone. When I looked in the mirror the next morning, my face was swollen but I told myself that from now on, I was in charge of my life. I realized that without trust and equality of partnership, our marriage could not work.

When I took the metro to go to work the next day, I felt strong and secure. I suddenly saw the world through different eyes and somehow had an answer to every question or doubt that crossed my mind. I discovered new possibilities, new ways out, wherever I looked. I had an incredible impression of being free. When I let my decision be known to my husband he lost control completely and started to cry. The hardest part was yet to come. Was I going to be able to follow up on my decision? I was swaying in between two different points of view. When I considered my decision as a tearing apart of our family, I did not want to pursue my plan. When I thought of the reality of the circumstances which were making my life miserable, I wanted to get divorced.

I tried to explain my motives to Horst as well as I could. He promised me yet again that he would change but the way we hurt each other emotionally had to come to an end. Neither of us was getting better, only more frustrated. We were about to celebrate our son's second birthday but now we had to discuss who would have custody of him in the future. After a remarkably calm discussion, we agreed that I would take care of Jan whilst Horst would have full visiting rights. Only a few days after that, he moved out. On our son's birthday he came to say hello and left after five minutes. I sat alone with my little boy and his birthday cake and got a bitter taste of what it would be like in the following months.

After everything was put in order with the divorce papers, Horst's sadness turned into anger. While in the first few weeks he had still given some money to support us, he now stopped all support and did not show up at all to see his son. My short-term employment at the hospital was coming to an end and I went to request government aid. My contract with the record company did include the possibility of advances but I was too inexperienced to take advantage of it. I believed that I would only get myself into debt because I didn't understand that these advances would only be reimbursable from future sales and not from me personally.

In October 1990, we continued to work on the album after having stopped for a couple of months because of the studio scheduling. The people there were little surprised about my news and told me that things were going to work out fine. I needed to hear that because I had become quite concerned about my ability to take care of a child alone. After the recordings for my album were finished, I didn't hear from the studio for about two months. Again I questioned whether or not I had any real chance to succeed in showbiz.

The government was still not organized in the East so that I was told I would have to wait some weeks before getting any support payments. My husband was refusing to make any payments by then and my parents were not in a position to offer real financial help since they were both unemployed at that time. Considering the situation, which was shared by many other single parents, I could not afford to be choosy and had to look for a job where I could make some money fast.

So I began to clean offices in West Berlin. I was not really allowed to work since I had requested government support but there was no alternative. Working two hours a day, making five hundred marks a month was not a bad deal but it was nevertheless on the borderline of serious financial trouble. Now I was at least able to organize my budget and just make it through. I was not sure whether or not the situation was going to improve or if this was the beginning of the end. Like everyone else from the former society, I had never had to face these kinds of circumstances and, inexperienced and worried about the future, I struggled from day to day.

At that time my sister was still in college and shared an apartment with her boyfriend. Sometimes they came to visit me and seeing them drive around in their car and sharing their love, while I was facing the daily struggle alone with my child, made my loneliness seem even more terrible. More than once I came close to giving up my divorce.

This type of transition was the hardest part of the change, in my opinion. Many people found themselves on the edge of survival. Often in the morning, when it was still dark, I would sit in the bus going to West Berlin and look at the tired faces of the people.

Looking at my own face in the window, I could see the dark rings around my eyes. Scared by this unfamiliar apparition, I would look down and ask myself if this reunion wasn't going to consume us. I fought against the feeling of being forgotten and disadvantaged. Yet, I held out against becoming still more sad and discouraged. It seemed obvious that the workers of the East had become the losers in this political game. There was no way that I was going to accept that for myself. Faith had become my flag some years ago and I was not willing to let go of it. So I turned my head back to the window and smiled.

My parents were sorry to hear about my decision to get divorced but could understand that it was probably the right thing to do. They were far more concerned about how I was going to earn a living for my son and myself. Both of them had lost their jobs and the chances for reintegration in the workforce of the new society were small. Their age didn't favor them but it was particularly because of their former work that they now had very little hope of obtaining more.

Before my decision to get divorced they had been able to afford a new car from their savings. No matter how tough the times had become, they were easier to handle with some kind of an asset. This car gave them a feeling of independence. I was glad to see that they had finally allowed themselves some material comfort. It also made it easier for us to get together.

My grandmother, who received a good pension from the new government, supported us whenever she could. She had had to stop working in her forties because of a problem with her legs and had been more or less at the mercy of everybody else. Now she was the one able to provide. It was another one of the strange ironies of that time. That gave her a lot of self confidence and she found new motivation for her life. Pulling together as a family, we were able to put ourselves through some tight budgets in the times to come.

Still, I had to carry on with all the responsibility on my own. My son and I built a strong relationship together during this period. As little as he was he sometimes put his arms around me when he saw me cry. I felt an incredible amount of warmth from this little guy which helped me to be strong. The winter of 1991 was lonely and cold. I was hardly able to warm up the apartment and one Saturday in January, I couldn't get out of bed. A bad cold must have come over me. I couldn't muster enough energy to fetch the coal from the basement or to call my parents. In those moments, I was not sure at all if I had done the right thing. I had difficulty talking and was trying to tell my son how much I loved him. He played silently for hours in front of my bed, coming to me from time to time to give me a hug.

It was an important experience for me to realize that I wasn't alone, that I had a wonderful son. It opened my eyes to the positive side of our life together. I guess I had developed quite an amount of negativity by then which might have put too much pressure on Jan. He was surely not the one to blame and yet, I wasn't always able to surround him with the happiness he deserved.

Today I wonder why I didn't go to a neighbor to ask for help to get to a doctor. Anyway, the following day I felt much better and did not really understand what could have come over me the day before. I did not have any more signs of a cold and was able to go to work after the weekend. After this brief physical breakdown, my self-confidence returned. I knew Jan and I could make it together. We had overcome a difficult situation by ourselves and it could only get better.

During the day my son went to the daycare which gave me a chance to concentrate on my music after work. I had managed to get hold of another used piano. During the winter of 1990-1991, I felt an incredible urge to write songs. I sat at my piano and without really knowing how to play it, I started to compose melodies while playing the harmonies and rhythms on the keyboard. Even though I did not know how to write lyrics, I felt that I had to say something, so I expressed it all in melodies which later became an important part of my first album in Canada.

Since I had no telephone at home, I gave the number of the place where I worked, to my record company. One morning while I was passing the vacuum-cleaner, I was called to the phone and my producer told me that they were going to do a video with me. After all the time that had passed since I had last heard from them, I thought they had forgotten me. The incredible news lifted my optimism sky high and I can mark this as the point where things really started to get better. Even though the video itself did not have such an overwhelming concept or very great art direction, it was still a good experience for me and gave me new drive.

The company I cleaned the offices for was a job-broking organization and I started thinking that a secretarial post would suit me very well. I liked to imagine myself as such, thinking to make it my way of earning a living for the time being. I felt comfortable with the idea of answering the telephone, writing letters, having my own desk as a receptionist, making coffee and wearing high heels. At least that was my idea of the profession.

First I had to find a way to learn how to type. In the waiting room, there was a desk installed with a typewriter for people who came for job interviews. They used it to give an example of their ability, by typing a certain text within ten minutes. I told my boss about my plan and asked her if I could use this machine to practice on after I finished work. She gave me the permission and I went straight out to buy myself a typing guide for beginners.

From then on I sat every day for an hour and slowly tapped in letter by letter, using the technique in the book. I continued this for a time by myself, then I found an announcement for an evening school in West Berlin which was starting a type-writing course. I thought that would be a quicker way to learn. The inscriptions were done on a Saturday and my sister came to my place to take care of Jan while I was gone.

Arriving at the school, I was amazed at how many hundreds of people, both young and old, had showed up until I understood that there was only one inscription day per semester for all the available courses. After four hours of standing, sitting and even lying down in the line, I arrived at the front and was glad to hear that there was still space available in the course. I had to pay about eighty marks for the whole course and needed to go twice a week for a period of three months.

We were heading into the month of March by then and six months had passed since I requested government support. One day I got the long awaited letter that my payments were finally being transferred to my bank account. The extra cash that I received was enough to follow up on my next plan. I was going to acquire a driver's license. Shortly after I stopped working as a cleaning woman, I got a telegram from the record company. That particular evening I was coming back with my parents from their place and when I read the telegram I literally jumped in the air. I was being asked to sing the backing vocals for a Canadian artist who was arriving soon to do an album in Berlin. My parents were as surprised as I was and they argued, in a funny way, as to which of them was going to read the telegram first. They spent a good while overcoming their disbelief and let themselves be hugged by me over and over again. To sing with an artist who came from another continent was one of the greatest things that could ever happen to me!

Berlin Hansa Studio, March 1991

The same evening I received the telegram my parents had to return home. At least I had my little boy, who was at that time two and a half, to share my happiness with. The recording session was scheduled for the following week. I could not wait for the time to move ahead. The winter was leaving us and the spring sun was already beginning to warm the air. I was completely taken over by the famous spring fever and felt that something extra special was going to happen. The months of waiting and struggling transformed themselves slowly but surely into a time of progress and new directions.

Finally the day came when I was supposed to meet the Canadian. I did not know anything about him except that he played the guitar and wrote his own songs.

I arrived at the studio in a state of total excitement, of which my red ears were a clear proof. The foreign star hadn't yet finished dinner in the restaurant on the first floor so we all sat waiting for him to enter the studio. When the door finally opened, I looked in curious expectation at the man who entered. Everybody gave him a tumultuous welcome. I was surprised to see a man somewhere in his forties, bearded, not tall but strong-looking. After greeting each other, during which moment I almost broke my tongue trying to speak English, he started talking to his producer. It had been seven years since I had last practiced the basics of English at school and it seemed to have left me completely. I couldn't follow any of their conversation. The only thing I picked up was that his name was Pierre.

While they were conferring, I sat watching him talk. I used to have a certain prejudice against men with beards. My mother helped me feel that way by saying that all the food sticks in there. I had never had any contact with a bearded man before which is partly explained by the fact that most of the people I knew worked for the army, where no beards were allowed. It somehow didn't occur to me that I might ever get involved with one. Yet, watching him very intensely, I could see no trace of any forgotten morsels of food, even though he had just come back from dinner. The passing of this odd examination caused me a good deal of satisfaction. I began to observe his appearance with much more pleasant feelings and discovered that I liked the sound of his low voice.

When I realized that he was looking at me with curious eyes, I was caught by surprise to find my heart set on fire. After a little while we went into the sound studio to record his song. I was amazed to see how well our voices blended together even though I had some trouble reading the English lyrics. More than once I mixed up the words, which gave us a reason to have a good laugh. I needed that, as I was pretty high emotionally at the time. The technicians had given us only one microphone and at one point our knees touched. I found myself giving him a sidelong glance and for one brief moment our eyes met. Were we thinking the same thing? On the other side of the studio window, I could see the faces of the producers and technicians who were having fun watching us. At one point they told us over the intercom that they could see the steam of passion surrounding us. Pierre and I smiled at each other and I realized that it made me feel very good.

After the first song we took a break and went to sit down. It was strange at first because neither of us could express ourselves with words that the other could understand. He showed interest in speaking German so we sat trying to develop our first conversation. I decided to write down the lyrics of one of my album songs, which he told me he liked a lot. I began to translate it to him into German while he listened to what I said and watched how I said it with the greatest of interest.

It didn't take us too long to get to our first kiss. Naturally, in the very same moment someone walked in and surprised us. In the instant which followed, I suddenly noticed that he had a ring on his finger which I hadn't seen before. I was dumbstruck. How could it be that this man in whom I had so much interest, was unavailable? I had no intention of being his mistress for one night so I asked him about it point blank. He was very happy to tell me that he had been thinking of divorce for quite a while. This story from a man five thousand miles away from his wife did not convince me much but I had to at least give him the benefit of the doubt. Yet it was reason enough to put a brake on the passion I was feeling. I also felt sympathy for his wife and tried to imagine myself in her place, knowing that I could not accept to be cheated on.

Although I was not yet able to judge whether he was speaking the truth or not, I still could not deny my own feelings. There was something so pure and sincere about our connection and my intuition confirmed to me that it would be sensible to hold on to the magic we seemed to be sharing. We didn't know it then but we were also sharing the same worry. Would we lose sight of each other straight away, considering the fact that we lived on different continents? The distance probably made us build an even stronger emotional bond. I think that unconsciously, we knew we would have to work harder to keep such an unlikely couple together in the long run.

When the session was over and I was about to leave, Pierre jumped up and anxiously asked for my address. He didn't know that I was coming back the next evening to continue the recording. The producer explained the situation to him. I was flattered that he seemed to care enough to keep track of me and told him that I wanted to see him again too.

The next evening, when we arrived at the studio, we started right where we had left off. The connection was now even stronger. It was as if an invisible cord was tying us together. The album was being finished that night and as usual at the end of a production, the studio team sat and drank champagne. Pierre and I exchanged our addresses. He sat on my lap and I felt so secure, being almost buried underneath him. Neither of us wanted to let go of this warmth. We just kind of glued ourselves together every step of the way.

A grey morning started to climb its way through the

black of the night. It was soon time to say goodbye. He took my hand and put a bracelet around my wrist. He said I should not forget his presence somewhere in the world. Pierre and I looked in each others' eyes and it was clear; he was going to join me on my way home to extend our being together as long as possible. He called a taxi and we were suddenly on our way to Hennigsdorf. It was his first journey to the eastern part of Germany. In the taxi we sat as close together as possible and, as we passed over a bridge, we saw the sun rising over the city like a red fire-ball. Its colour advertised the arrival of a beautiful day and it seemed to us that it was also the symbol of a wonderful beginning.

As we came into Hennigsdorf, Pierre felt right away that he was in the Eastern sector because of the streets which were unpaved in certain places. They were built with rough stones which made the cars stumble along rather than drive. Further on, he took notice of the houses that all looked like one another, cloaked in the early morning light in their uniform greyness. He said that just a little colour would make everything much more friendly. I found that to be a great idea and wondered why nobody here had thought of it before. Just looking at my own experience made me realize that getting used to something can keep us from changing it.

Besides these few observations, he kept further criticism to himself. He did not want to appear as the spoiled Westerner who had come here to show off. He showed a great deal of respect for the background I came from and admitted that it can't have been so bad after all, judging by the person he was then starting to fall in love with. For my part, I was very excited about being in the company of a Canadian with whom I shared a great deal of common feelings. In the context of that sleepy little town, it was an extraordinary situation which I felt like broadcasting out the car window to the whole world.

From the first day onwards, I felt an immense growth in my self esteem, just from being by his side. His presence opened my eyes to another point of view on life: a power point of view. He made everything look so simple that it was contagious. I began to see things in a positive light and started learning to feel more relaxed and in control of my life. From this one short visit of his, I understood so much about how I could make things work for myself. It all had to do with self confidence, with not being afraid of life or other people. I saw him finding solutions to everything because he had decided to be in charge. I asked myself why I should not be able to become like that too.

After spending the day in Hennigsdorf he had to go back to Berlin because he had a plane to catch for Canada the next morning. The circumstances of the past three days had been pretty unusual and led us into a somewhat funny state of mind. After he had brought me all the way out to Hennigsdorf to say goodbye, I decided to accompany him back to Berlin! We were happy to discover that we had a certain sense of humour in common and arriving in Berlin he offered once again to take me back to Hennigsdorf. I'm just kidding! He called another taxi to take me home and it was really the time to say goodbye.

After Pierre left for Canada, I lived from the memories of his ways and tried to extend the sense of power that he had awoken inside of me. Situations that used to cost me quite a lot of effort suddenly became easier to handle. Things like shopping on a tight budget or being a single mom, no longer exerted the same pressure on me. As I came to understand my own worth, I became more and more a part of the world and less and less alienated from it. From this point on I began to let go of life as an anxious struggle and learned to approve of myself instead of seeking the approval of others. Yet, I got only a taste of what it feels like to use the potential that is offered to us every day, instead of feeling victimized by circumstances that I believed I could do nothing about.

Finding myself alone in the evening after saying goodbye to Pierre, I felt as if I had dreamed it all. It seemed so far from the reality I had known until just a few days ago. Looked at logically, it was totally out of context and impossible. Only the great happiness I felt and the sweet pain of longing which made my stomach gently turn, proved to me that there was something happening for real. Again, it took me quite some time to get my thoughts in order. Eventually I was able to classify this underlying anticipation that I had felt for several weeks. I constantly sensed a burning feeling inside, like a small bright flame that was drawing my attention to something special that was about to happen. Then when it did happen, it was as if I had been sitting all the time on a sleeping volcano which had suddenly broken out and thrown me high up towards the sky.

The next day I sat down to write a letter. First, I wrote down in German what I wanted to say. Then, with the greatest of efforts, I set about translating it into English. I needed to look in the dictionary for at least every second word. When I mailed the letter I put an airmail sticker on it and just doing that small thing made me so proud of this adventurous liaison. I was amazed and touched by the fact that such a distance could be involved in finding love. I did worry a little bit as to whether or not Pierre would still think of me and if so, if he would be interested in receiving a love-letter from me. I wondered if our meeting might not have been just a chance and meaningless hiatus in the round of his regular life. Could it really have meant as much to him as it had to me?

While my first airmail letter was winging its way across the ocean, I went on with the theoretical course necessary to obtain a driver's license. After about two weeks, on a Saturday, I had to attend a lesson in first-aid training. My mother came to visit me over the weekend and took care of Jan for me at the same time. When I returned home there was a surprise waiting for me. My mother was mysteriously holding a letter in her hands. With a smile on her lips and without a word, she handed it over to me and when I saw that it came from Canada I had to sit down at once. My hands had begun to shake so much, I could hardly open the letter. Inside of me there was still a struggle going on to know if this letter might not be a mere note from him, apologizing for having awoken false hopes. Or would it be a positive answer to the letter I had sent to him?

When I started to look at the letter, I realized I could not understand too much but I kept seeing one word I thought I knew. It was written over and over again: *love, love, love*. My eyes flew over the lines and it took me a few seconds to realize that I had received a love-letter as well. Tears of joy ran down my face. Even my mother could not repress a wave of emotion that seemed to have gotten to her too.

The retaining wall which I had built around my feelings to protect them from getting hurt, vanished all of a sudden. My insecurity about our continuing contact transformed itself into a clear confirmation that similar feelings existed on both sides. Looking at the mailing date, I realized that he had sent this letter almost at the same time as I had sent mine. So it couldn't even be a direct answer to the one I had sent. This made it infinitesimally more important to me. As soon as I had a chance, I sat down to reply and was happy to see that I was already getting a little bit better with my English.

It was April then and since a few days I had been desperate to get out of my apartment. I had made the upsetting discovery that there were more vermin in that place. A spider with a body size of about an inch was sitting on the wall in the kitchen. It seemed to me as though they were getting bigger every time I found a new one. I thought I had already seen the worst and hoped for a moment that I was hallucinating.

Anxiously, I called my neighbor who came and rescued me with an expression of the greatest disgust on his own face at the sight of that animal. From that moment on, I swore to myself I would not stay one more day there. My neighbor offered to move me into the apartment of his girlfriend who was going to move in with him. I was particularly grateful for this offer and considered it as a lucky escape from the nightmare of all these bugs.

The arrangements were made the next day and I offered to leave my bedroom set behind if I could move in immediately. As fast as I could, I organized a moving truck and asked my parents to help me move my things, including my piano. They had already helped move the piano into my old place once and were exhausted just by the memory of it. Yet they could not refuse to help me another time because they did not want to see their grandson and me in this terrible apartment anymore either. My neighbor was also a great help and altogether, I was able to move out in less than three days. Even though the move occurred without the knowledge or permission of the government, which we should have had, I didn't care as much about possible trouble as I did about getting out of there. Nobody was ever going to put me back in there. I was leaving, period!

Whilst packing my remaining things, I took a last look in the mailbox and found another long-awaited letter from Pierre. It contained a cassette with a new song of his on it with lyrics that were exclusively built using lines from my album titles. It was well put together and really was the nicest love song I'd ever heard, especially as it was written for me. My spontaneous decision to move, as well as the determination with which I pursued my plan, were greatly encouraged by my new relationship. Pierre really made me believe in myself. In his letter, he also let me know that he was returning to Germany in June and that was the greatest news of all.

The new place I had moved into was in a little city called Velten, about fifteen minutes away from Hennigsdorf by car. I was incredibly lucky that it was an apartment with central heating and hot water. It was a hundred times more friendly than the other place and the area the apartment block was built in was tidy. This place was also reserved for members of the army. I should mention that the socialist army was gradually being transformed into part of the western army. Many army people had lost their jobs but many others had agreed to work for their former enemies. There were many such bizarre things happening then. It reminds me of a German saying: '*Who's bread I eat, that's whose song I'll sing.*'

I knew that I wasn't going to be able to stay for long in that place. The government wouldn't take too long to find out about it, especially since empty apartments were rare and reoccupied fast. Finally, the girl whose place it was, was obliged to announce her movement to the police as every person in Germany has to do. Still, I had managed to stay there for over a month which gave me a needed break from the discomfort of the other place and a chance to enjoy taking a bath without having to heat it with coal two hours in advance. As well, it was nice to have had a warm and cozy place that held no unpleasant surprises for me.

Once I got an unexpected visitor whom I recognized as one of my producers from the time before the wall had come down. He had managed to find out where I lived and was now standing there, offering to do a project with me. The conditions in my artist's contract with Musicolor in Berlin, did not allow me to accept but I was very flattered that he had made all those efforts to find me. It took my self-confidence a stage further.

When it finally became impossible to conceal the fact of our various moves, I went with the girl whose flat it had been, to the government building from which the distribution of apartments for our area was directed. We explained the situation and I was told that I had to move out because they needed the place for a member of the army. Anxious once again about the turn of fate, I went to see another person in the same building.

I begged him to find me a habitable place to live in and he finally turned up a small apartment in Hennigsdorf. It was on the same street as I had lived before but was on the second floor. I was so happy when I got out of there with a paper that gave me the legal right to move into that place. When I got back to Hennigsdorf, I saw that the apartment had a nice position with a neat garden in front. Inside I could see the difference to the other place. I called my parents to tell them the good news that I had to move again.

They were glad to see my valid rental contract but swore to themselves that they were not going to move the piano another time. They came again to support me with the condition that I'd allow them to break the piano apart. By then I was so relieved at having found a better place in which to live, that I didn't care too much about the rest. I just wanted to get things in order and finished with. Again I ordered a moving truck to move all my things. People were already at work, renovating my new apartment.

When my parents came over, they started to take the piano apart with a passion that was quite surprising. Not only did they destroy it completely stick by stick, I think that with every string they severed, they excised a piece of their frustration, as if the piano itself had been a rival to the plans they had had for me. They hammered against the wooden sides with a passion as if every stroke was an attempt to eliminate the musical ambition of their daughter! Furthermore they seemed to really enjoy carrying the piano outside in small pieces instead of having to dislocate their arms while trying to move this 'monster' around. They did not even want to let me help and worked in a hurry as if they were afraid I might change my mind.

Feeling a little sentimental about the whole scene, I went out with my son to buy lunch. The noise of the hammer crashing down on the piano and the final but powerful "zmmmm" of each string being cut attracted the attention of the neighbors. They hadn't seen much of me, of course. By the time I had moved in, I was already moving out again. They were probably even more confused when they saw the same people who had brought the piano in with the severest of efforts, just weeks earlier, carrying it outside in pieces.

While all the moving was going on, I finished my typing course and started to think about what I was going to do with this new accomplishment. I went to the job office and asked what the possibilities were of obtaining a job other than teaching. Normally people were supposed to stay in their profession so it was a difficult position for everyone concerned. It would have been easier had I wanted to gain extra qualifications or change direction as a teacher. Most courses were of two years duration and paid for by the government, so it had to have some kind of connection to my existing profession.

I couldn't stand the idea of being stuck in the teaching profession forever and expressed my fears to the employee who was in charge of my file. I showed her the paper I had received from my typing course and in the end, she did seem to know a way out. She told me to come back in a few days which at least gave me a glimmer of hope. When I returned to her office a week later she was able to offer me a choice of two courses. One of them was to become an accountant and the other to become a secretary specializing in legal work. It didn't take me long to make up my mind and I gratefully filled in the application for the secretarial course.

There was only one condition to which I had to find a solution. The program called for two days per week of theory at school and three days of practical work in a lawyer's office. Therefore I needed to go and find a lawyer who was willing to accept me as a student and to support my development. The school I would have to go to was in Berlin but I decided to start my search for a lawyer closer to home. I didn't have any luck in the former Eastern part since there were not many lawyers to start with and the few that I found were not open to my request. So I began to look through the newspapers and called the various offices which were advertising a vacancy. That tack didn't work either, since most of them were looking for a secretary who already had training and others had just accepted a new student.

I decided to go to Berlin and get an interview with someone myself. I took the bus and metro into the city and then just walked along the streets, looking for lawyers' shingles. At one office I had an interview right away but was told by letter a few days later that the place had been filled by someone else. The next time I went back to Berlin, I headed to the biggest street in the centre of the city, called the Kurfurstendamm. It is a very commercial street and as I walked along it, I saw a lawyer's sign on every third door. It was hard for me to decide where to stop so I divided the potential candidates into categories for myself. I considered things like the sound of the lawyer's name, the look of the building and the distance to the metro.

Finally I stopped in front of a building which corresponded in general to my ideas and was only five minutes away from the nearest metro station. Having climbed the stairs, I had some trouble opening the huge door which barred my way but I finally got in and made my way to the reception. Here I was received with curious looks, as though nobody had ever been there on such an errand before. After informing the receptionist of my intentions, I was asked to wait a minute while she went in to talk to her boss.

Shortly after that I was ushered into an office where a friendly-looking man in his thirties greeted me. He told me he was the firm's junior lawyer and, although he would need to discuss the matter with his father, he was personally open to the idea. They hadn't planned on taking on a student but the idea of having someone around to help out with the work appealed to him. He appreciated the fact that they wouldn't need to pay anything because I was going to be paid by the government from within the program I was doing. Since his father was absent, he asked me to wait a few more days and said they would invite me back for a further interview. When I left the office that day, I had a very good feeling about the people I had just met and about the place itself.

The date of Pierre's return to Germany was coming closer and closer. It was then the beginning of June and I awaited his return impatiently. I asked myself how things would turn out this time since we had met for only three days and had not seen each other for more than two months. Both of us were haunted by the oddly familiar impression that we were meeting someone for the first time and yet that we had known each other for years. We seemed to be locked in a private time zone of our own. It was a strange combination of novelty mixed with a sense of déjà vu.

I had written to him about the renovation of my new apartment which was not going to be finished for his arrival so he organized a room in the building which the studio had reserved for guests. While the work was going on at my new place, I stayed with my parents in Frankfurt (Oder). They followed this love story with some incredulity and were dying of curiosity to see this Canadian man. They had never met an English-speaking person before and I was so glad about the fact that finally, my father would be unable to involve someone in a political argument. I will never forget the look my father gave me when I told him that my new friend was only ten years younger than he was. He looked at me and could only say:

"Pina..." and having said that, his mouth stayed open for a while. My parents have a hard time taking people seriously if they are under forty. Pierre's age increased their respect for our relationship at once.

When I went to meet Pierre, it was the first time that I had ever been to an airport. I took the train from my parents' town to go to Berlin and was very nervous about getting lost on my way. Even though he sent me all the information I needed in order to find him, (including a drawing of a plane!), my hands were wet and my mouth was dry as I neared the destination. I asked myself why some things are exactly the opposite of what they should be when we get nervous. Jan was very excited at the thought of seeing some real planes and I had to hold on to him tightly in order not to lose sight of him.

Finally Pierre came out of the gate with a crowd of people and I was a little embarrassed at the way he hugged me in front of all of them. With one arm I hung on to Jan while I wrapped the other around Pierre's neck. He said in German that he was tired but very happy to be here:

"*Ich bin müde, aber sehr glücklich hier zu sein.*" I was shy about expressing my feelings in public and having people watch me kiss. Before I even realized that he was waiting to be complimented about his efforts at speaking German, I had pulled him away from the gate. Wondering what the rush was all about, he repeated his German phrase to me but I was still too nervous to reply as I should have. Instead, I could only produce this badly formed English sentence:

"Yeah, me also." From there things cooled down and I began to notice how much more nervously I was acting compared to him. Later I found out that he had been pretty nervous too. He just didn't show it in his movements. I was jumping about all over the place.

It was strange to feel so familiar right away, even though we hardly knew each other. My son obviously felt very comfortable in Pierre's presence and could not stop reaching up to touch the interesting beard. We joined him when he went to exchange Canadian dollars and then to rent a car. These were events that I participated in proudly. I admired how he handled what were to me, strange procedures and I was nonplussed by the super friendly attention of the people who served him. I had never had an experience like it.

Afterwards we headed back to my parents home where we were invited for dinner. It was a good occasion for everyone to meet. At the same time we had to pick up a little bed for my son, since there was only one available for us in the studio apartment. Arriving at my parents' place, my mother's face was red with excitement. She was pretty mixed up when Pierre took her in his arms. My heart danced when I saw her little figure almost disappearing in Pierre's embrace; I was so proud to be able to introduce him to her. My father wasn't home when we got there and since Pierre was very tired, my mother offered him a chance to get some rest. When he went to lay down my mother and I went into the kitchen. Try as she might, she didn't know what to say to me except that he seemed very nice, yes, very nice.

It was funny to see my father's face when he got home and heard that Pierre was meditating. This was something he had never heard of except in the context of charlatans and bogus doctors. I had rarely seen him being so respectful as he was trying to be then.

We all knew that Pierre had been on his journey for about fifteen hours and granted him his peace. It also gave my mother a chance to come to her senses. The whole situation was so out of the ordinary for our family that we all needed some time to digest it. The strangest thing for them was, perhaps, that this was the first time that they had met someone from the western world in person. They were not even going to be able to communicate with him but they had to welcome him into their family.

Still they managed to let go of any prejudices and looked forward to his introduction with great sympathy. There was an undeniable feeling of pride because, in the context of recent social changes, many people had faced an immense struggle to find a new beginning. That idea, of starting afresh, was finally starting to permeate through my parents' house. Even though I had rejected the thought of going to Canada at that time, the atmosphere in our family was enriched with general hope and motivation for life.

Pierre had only been resting for about twenty minutes when he opened the door with a happy hello. My father almost ran over to introduce himself and then poured an incredible amount of pleasant words upon him, almost forgetting that Pierre wasn't able to understand a thing. Since there wasn't much chance of small-talk before dinner, we soon decided to sit down and eat.

The dinner table was set very nicely and Pierre was regaled with a German specialty: potato salad and sausages. It was a delicious meal during which my parents giggled like kids when they heard Pierre talking in his strange language. My father almost made a knot in his tongue while awkwardly trying to pronounce some of the words. To show he was in the spirit of things, he kept on throwing in the few words of Russian he knew or tried to speak German words with an English accent, as if Pierre might understand some of that better. It was the same approach I had tried years ago, when I marched beside the Russian soldiers.

Meanwhile, I was feeling very important for once, since I had the role of translator and my parents had to depend on me in order to communicate. It was an uproarious table with Jan the one laughing the loudest, as if he knew exactly what was going on. After dinner Pierre, Jan and I all left for the studio apartment in Berlin because the next day he was scheduled to work there. We planned on coming back for the weekend to visit my parents again. The studio apartment was made of an entrance, a bathroom and one bedroom.

The following week was particularly special because of the fact that all three of us had to get along in the tiny space available. It actually helped us very much to build stronger links together. While we had remained far apart we had not been able to see things clearly and it was now becoming clearer and clearer that Pierre and I had completely fallen in love. The magic we felt from the very beginning had not faded and our emotional bond was incredibly strong.

During this time we also went to the North Sea in the former eastern part of the country. After our four hour drive, we had a cold reception from the local people when we tried to find a place for the night. Pierre was amazed to see how many hotels were closed due to bankruptcy. He thought that the opposite ought to be happening after all the big changes. The general impression about the wall coming down was more positive than reality proved it to be. When we asked for directions and people heard Pierre speaking in English, almost everyone we met acted as though they were repulsed by our presence. It was as if they were afraid to have more strangers coming in, to further disrupt their already disordered lives.

As a Westerner, Pierre only then started to appreciate the other side of the social changes, about which many people in the East were not at all enthusiastic. Many of them could only see that they were having to give up old ground. The benefits, if any, were still hidden by the new round of hardships.

It was not warm at the time we went to the seaside; the water temperature was eleven degrees Celsius and the wind pretty strong. Yet, Pierre and I decided to go for a swim to prove our bravery to each other. It was the fastest bath I have ever taken and after only a few seconds, both of us ran out of the water as if we had seen a shark.

The next day we went back to Frankfurt (Oder) where we spent the weekend together. It was amazing to see how respectfully my parents treated both Pierre and me. We had an exciting time and it took quite a while to get little Jan to go to bed. When it got late, my mother went to bed as well, while the three of us kept on celebrating life. We spent all the time talking and laughing and I could feel incredible happiness and love coming from my father, things that I had missed for such a long time. After the wall came down, he stopped playing the accordion and was not yet at the point where he was willing to take it up again. In the initial period, he had seen no reason to celebrate and for the first time since the drama of 1989, I heard him laugh loudly and freely that night.

At one stage, Pierre ran out of cigarettes. That was extraordinary since it had been my father, who had stopped smoking ten years earlier, and I, who normally never smoke at home, who had smoked them all. It was a night for strange happenings. Pierre produced some cigars from a pocket somewhere and offered them to my father and I. I knew my father's opposition to smoking was normally fierce, so I was amazed that he could tolerate seeing me smoke with hardly a comment. I guess he couldn't say too much as he had broken his own rule for the evening as well. Still it was unusual for him not to criticize. When I took a cigar and heard my father only ask mildly:

"You too?" I could not believe it. Truly, such changes were being wrought then as we had never dreamed of.

The three of us went outside on the balcony so we wouldn't stink the apartment out with the strong smell of cigars. I was overwhelmed at seeing my father suddenly look years younger. His face seemed free of sorrow and he wore an expression of cheerful ferocity. It made me so happy to see him like that. For the first time in my life, I felt some genuine real relief from his overprotective ways which had so often stopped me from making my own decisions. I felt accepted as a human being who, although I might sometimes do crazy things, was allowed to control her own life. I suppose because of my conditioning, I expected a subsequent comment about it all but my father didn't criticize a thing, not the next day, nor even after Pierre had left. He kept on talking about the good time we had all had together, which was very uncommon for this man who would normally never allow anyone to enjoy simple pleasures. It was a revelation to me.

We had to go back to Berlin because Pierre was leaving for Canada again soon. Altogether he stayed for ten days and the day before his departure I found a letter in my mail-box from the lawyer in Berlin. I was asked to come for an interview at which time they would let me know whether or not I was going to be accepted. This letter alone was already so affirmative that I fell around Pierre's neck before he knew what I was celebrating. He already knew about my application and was pleased to hear that things were going in a positive direction.

As I took him to the airport the next day, I carried my heart like a heavy rock. To hear that he was coming back in six weeks was a big relief, yet it didn't relieve the sadness I was feeling at this point. It was a strange mixture of being happy about loving each other and sad that we could not be together for real. It was such a delicate balance. For the next eight months, Pierre returned to Germany every six weeks, staying for periods of ten days.

The day for the job interview came and I was asked to start right away. There was a very positive side to working in this office. Pierre was able to contact me by fax or telephone which seemed to dramatically decrease the distance between us. I enjoyed going to work every day, being in the middle of all the action. It made me feel good about myself and I also got along well with the other people.

Meanwhile, school had started but from then on, Jan and myself had to cope with a difficult schedule. I would leave the house at seven o'clock in the morning and get back at six in the evening, so it did not leave much time for my son. The stress of trying to manage the schedule, which included homework at night, made it very tough to be a good mom. I was worried that Jan would feel bad about spending so many hours at the daycare. Neither of us were used to that kind of pressure and I soon caught a bad cold that I couldn't shake off for weeks.

Hennigsdorf, September 1991

When Pierre came back to Germany again, he found us in a state of exhaustion. Jan had also become sick and had such a strong cough, that it forced him to vomit. I was concerned about his condition and Pierre drove us to the hospital.

Maybe what then occurred was partly caused by the general stress of the situation. After we had been in the hospital waiting-room for about an hour, Pierre asked me to find out how long we might still have to wait. He wanted to know if he had time to pick up something to eat. This surprised me because I had been so used to waiting for things in the past, that it would never have occurred to me to do anything other than wait patiently for our turn. I had stopped asking questions like that years earlier because I had learned that it did no good. You would just be put down as being impatient and pushy.

Since I was very nervous about Jan, I didn't want to take the risk of getting unfriendly service. So I told Pierre just to be quiet and there was almost an argument on the spot. How could he know what lay behind my incautious words? How could I understand, straight away, that he was, in his own way, being naive about our system?

There were many other situations which caused misunderstandings because of the different way we had been brought up. We needed to get a lot more practice to be able to realize and identify certain situations, in order not to let them affect our communication negatively.

After two hours of waiting and then getting x-rays taken, my son was diagnosed with pneumonia. The news hit me like a rock. It was the first time Jan had been seriously ill and I didn't know how to deal with the helpless feeling I had, of being unable to relieve him from suffering. He had to stay in hospital for a full week, getting three injections of penicillin daily. It was the most terrible experience I had ever had as a mother, to have to leave my crying boy behind in an empty hospital room. The rules of the hospital did not allow me to stay with him for the night or to visit him whenever I wanted. That was another thing Pierre had a hard time understanding.

Besides the fact that Jan was seriously ill, I faced another financial problem similar to one I had had before when I needed state assistance. The government was still not able to adjust the speed of their actions to the speed of change in peoples' lives. I was once again put on hold with no monthly income, despite the fact that I was, supposedly, in a government program. At one point, my colleagues at work advised me to go and sit in the government office-building with my child and not to leave until I had a check in my hands. Pierre said he could hardly believe it when he saw how things were functioning, or not functioning, in the reunited Germany.

There was one good piece of news about then because my divorce was finally over and done with. The year of separation that every divorcing couple had to go through before the divorce became legal, had passed. In the meantime, I was also able to conclude a court action against Horst, by means of which he was ordered to pay alimony to help support Jan. Even though he signed for a fairly low amount based on a compromise we had made with regard to his ability to pay, he did not respect the agreement. He seized the opportunity to demonstrate his frustration about my decision to divorce him. His attitude confirmed my fears that there were far more important things to Horst than the support of his child and that I had made the right decision by divorcing him.

With the support of the courts, I was later able to collect an amount of money which also included the alimony he had refused to pay in months past. He had no longer been able to find a way around the court order against him. Once the regular payments from the government began to flow again, my financial situation improved drastically. I was finally able me to support myself independently. I was even able to plan on buying furniture and carpets for my apartment.

When Pierre came to visit us in the fall, we went to choose the things needed and together we established a nice looking apartment. By then, Jan had fully recovered from his illness. We had fun, as if we were arranging our own nest. Some while earlier, we had started to think of living together. It was clear that we needed to come to some kind of conclusion in our relationship. In the long run, it was not possible for either of us to keep on living under those conditions. As well, there was the incredible expense of plane tickets every time we wanted to see each other. We began to talk about the possibility of him moving to Germany, since I was rather averse to the idea of going to Canada. I had no idea of what it might be like, no notion on which to base the decision of leaving my own country. Besides, I had to think of Jan as well. I was not prepared to take a decision concerning my own future, if it was likely to compromise his. I wanted what was right for both of us.

I planned on building a solid base for my life by finishing school and learning a profession which would be recognized by the new society. Further, I was not comfortable with the thought of quitting since I felt it was better to finish the things that I started. I had taken the lesson I learned in college to heart. Pierre supported my opinion by saying that it would be less of a problem to move his business from one country to another, because he could operate it from anywhere in the world. He had in fact been thinking of opening an office in Germany anyway.

While I was at work each day, he began to make drawings of a house that he would eventually build after moving to Germany. When we could be together, we often went with the car to search for a nice place to live in the future. He also looked around to find an appropriate office for his business. He was tempted by the idea of living in the former eastern part but the problem was that there were hardly any telephone or fax connections available and this was of paramount importance to his business. So for a while, we got no further than making plans.

Christmas was on its way when Pierre invited me to visit him in Canada. Even though I had had a presentiment of something like this, I was nevertheless surprised when it was clear how soon it was going to come true. I could hardly imagine myself travelling to Canada because it seemed to lie so far outside my experience. That gave the voyage a touch of mystery and excitement as though I was about to begin the exploration of a new pathway in my life. An incredible energy caused events to start happening in my life which opened up the gate to a sort of wonderful garden. At times, the pace of things left me out of breath.

The day I left on the big trip, my parents took me to the airport. As we drove out, I had the uncanny feeling that I was close to having the answer to something very deep. It was as though I was on the verge of something really important, about which I was not yet able to clearly detect the meaning. My family was amazed to witness the different course my life had taken over the past few months. From having shortly before been pitied by my parents, I now saw that they were treating me with astonishment and respect. It was a big deal to them that I was to be the first of the family who would see another continent.

I was only leaving for one week during which time Jan stayed with his grandparents. To my consternation, they expressed their fear as to whether or not I would come back. Then I remembered that there were in fact many instances of people who had left their families after the wall came down. My parents' worries were understandable, when one considered the previous limitations of living in the GDR. The fall of the Iron Curtain suddenly exposed a world of apparently endless possibilities to our people. My parents, who had lived in the heartland of the GDR, found it especially difficult to come to terms with the changes.

So there I was, putting my feet on Canadian ground for the first time. I arrived on a cold winter's evening and everything was covered with snow. It was my first flight and I had listened anxiously throughout it for any odd sound that might come from the engines. It really didn't seem safe to me. Pierre came to meet me at the airport and I was at once happy and nervous. We were going to spend one week alone together and it seemed as if I had stepped into another world.

Thousands of snow crystals were sparkling in the dark. Sitting in the Jeep, heading north from the airport, I could see colorful lights everywhere. Multi-colored Christmas chains glimmered on houses and in trees. It was a celebration of happiness, lighting up the dark. Snow-covered mountains surrounded the country as if they wanted to shelter it and allow nothing to interfere with that peace. There were ski slopes dropping down from the mountains into the valley. We were going through a skier's paradise and the eye couldn't get enough of the countless lights radiating all over the ski-hills, offering a breath-taking view.

After a half hour drive we arrived at the house. To me it was the most beautiful of houses. It was made of reddish brown bricks and had a red roof. I find it significant that the houses in Canada are so colorful. People here are not afraid to put reds and greens and yellows on the rooves and walls. Beside these happy colors, the memory of my hometown seemed even more grey. Upon entering the house, I was welcomed with soft music, champagne and wood crackling in the fire place. Up to here I had seen this only in romantic movies and I was astonished by the cozy atmosphere created by it all.

Pierre added some more wood to the fire. For the first time I was able to see him in his own surroundings. For me, there is magic in the house and it is something Pierre has created. It is like a mirror of his emotions. He is a man of nature and his picture windows allow us to enjoy a vista of snow-covered forest.

The whole week was filled with 'firsts'. Pierre took me to do some snowshoeing and as we stamped through the deep snow, I was captivated by the clear colors of this northern landscape. In Frankfurt (Oder) the snow, when we had any, was usually grey, the same color as the sky.

On my birthday, which occurred during that week, I got to enjoy a sauna and a bubble bath at a spa in the mountains. When we returned to the house, there was a car parked in the driveway and Pierre gave me the impression that it had to be robbers. I got very agitated and told him to get the police and to take down the number of the license plate.

After doing so we drove off again but a few hundred meters further on, Pierre decided to return to the house. I was mixed up for I thought we were going to get the police. Now we saw a second car in front of the house and Pierre seemed to get more worried. For a moment it occurred to me that the Secret Service had come to get me because I was visiting a capitalist country. Even though I knew that things had changed permanently, I was haunted by the possibility that they might mysteriously have changed back. Such was the power of the old regime over us. No sort of subterfuge would have surprised me.

Pierre said he would go inside to check out what was going on. I was about to freak out completely and tried to stop him from putting himself in danger. Nevertheless, he entered the house and I followed him cautiously, prepared for the worst.

The door opened and some people began to sing Happy Birthday. I recognized them as two of Pierre's friends from the squash club who had come here before with their girlfriends. I was still a little confused but very flattered that Pierre had organized a party for me. I had never heard of a surprise party, so this one really worked! For dinner we had a cheese fondue which was also new to me. I put my fork in the cheese pot, thinking there was something else to be picked up. A little helpless, I tried to fish for whatever I expected to be in there and then impatiently asked:

"What the heck is this?" Everybody was quite amused, seeing me discover one new thing after the other. One couple had brought their huge dog which I was afraid of at first. Yet, after a few hours when we went for a walk on a frozen lake, I found myself playing and running with the dog over the ice. It was a week like that, from start to finish. I was beginning to discover what freedom could mean and it was exciting.

When I returned to Germany at the end of seven days, I seemed to fall from a wide cloud into a humid grey space, filled with morose faces and rain. When the plane took off from Mirabel, my heart wanted to stay on the ground. Canada had brought so much warmth to my heart that I thought it would freeze, just at the thought of Germany. I could feel something close to physical pain and was so mad with myself that I could not even make the effort to offer a smile to anybody. I just wanted to sleep and paralyze the sadness I was feeling. I could not see how I was to return to a normal life in Germany.

When I finally got to Berlin I felt like a stranger. What I saw there was so different from what I had experienced in Canada. I was totally depressed about facing what was for me, the cold reality of home. I had seen such a difference in the general way of living, in the mentality of the people, even in the landscape. When I entered my ice-cold apartment in Hennigsdorf, I thought I couldn't bare it any longer. I dropped onto the bed and slept for four hours. Unbelievably, when I woke up, I found yet more vermin in the bed. I dispatched them with the greatest frustration and then fell asleep again until the next morning.

I went to my parents' place to pick up my son. They were happy to see me back and tried hard to believe all the nice things that I told them. Happy as I had been to be in Canada, I had missed Jan very much and to take him in my arms again was the nicest thing about my return. I said to myself that if I would ever go again, I would take him with me.

After the weekend, I got straight back to the routine of working and going to school. I started to notice that I was not the only one who was frustrated about the way things were going. Many of the girls in the class were wondering what all the effort was for. We had all experienced standing in the rain with a paper qualification which had become worthless. We had worked hard for them, believing that it would provide us with security for life. It was hard to find the motivation to begin all over again but it was becoming daily more clear that there was no other choice.

January 1992 was a dark month in every way. I found it incredibly difficult to keep on with what I was doing. To know Pierre and the kind of life he was leading in Canada made it hard for me to accept my own life circumstances. I could not, nor did I want to, find reasons enough to justify the struggle. One of the things he taught me was that we do have the power to create the conditions we want to live in. More and more I thought about that and started to realize that I had to make a choice in order to change. Nobody was going to make that choice for me.

One day I came home from work and went down to the basement to get some coal. To my amazement, I found that someone had broken in and stolen a large part of my supply. I did not want to believe that someone could be so hardhearted as to take away the source of warmth from another person. Then again, I blamed the society for allowing social conditions to deteriorate so much, that people grew desperate and hurt each other. I was furious and went to the police to get help. They put a notice up in the neighborhood ordering whoever the thief was, to bring back my coals. They also advised me to change the lock on my coal locker. I didn't hear any more about it.

Another thing which contributed to my constant exhaustion, was a neighbor who unnerved the whole neighborhood with his loud music. I would often come home from work with headaches, wishing for nothing more than a little peace, I would open the door of the block and find more noise than ever. This went on almost daily and although people called the police several times, by the time they arrived the offender had always turned the volume down. The police felt powerless to do anything with our complaints because they had to hear the noise for themselves. It was not enough for them to have nearly a dozen witnesses, all of whom confirmed the situation and told them about their crying children who were getting no sleep.

I started to feel very discouraged about the number of situations in which the ordinary citizen was exposed to unfairness of all sorts, while the law seemed unable to defend his rights. The silly business of the loud music was like one more thorn in my side. I was going crazy watching the new society malfunction and my general fatigue with it all grew, the more I thought about a possible opportunity to change. Because I could see a way out, it was so much harder for me to accept this kind of struggle. As I thought about my efforts to obtain new qualifications, I suddenly realized that I was acting like a model who changes clothes to the liking of different customers. I tried listening carefully to what was bothering me inside and could literally see my frustration growing.

The next time Pierre came back to Germany, we went to look for a little keyboard that could stay at my apartment. All this time, we had planned on doing music together and he wanted to support me in my personal artistic development. We had trouble finding the right kind of thing and Pierre began to realize that Germany was quite a bit more expensive than Canada, in many regards. Without meaning anything else by it, he said in some frustration:

"What am I doing? I have all this stuff at home." All of a sudden, I was overtaken by a strong feeling of certainty. The situation of being unable to find an affordable keyboard was just there to help me see clearly. Together we had to realize the trouble we were going through, by trying to make things work under these complicated conditions.

I took Pierre by the hand and said that I needed to talk to him, right then and there. We went to the nearest restaurant which was more of a dark pub really but it didn't matter. It was wonderful to be sitting together in a warm place. Pierre looked at me expectantly while I stirred the milk in my coffee. Suddenly I looked up and told him that it would make sense for me to go to Canada.

He didn't look too surprised, I must say and he told me that he had privately been hoping for such a decision. I was glad that it was finally said and that we were both agreed on it. I took the time to explain to him the thought process I had gone through so that he clearly understood where I was coming from. After confirming with each other some major issues concerning my son, my work over there, the environment we would live in and so on, we took the final decision together. We were going to live as a family while I would also work for his company. He would hire me for my knowledge of the Russian language which would assist him to enter the Russian music market.

I cannot adequately describe the feelings of relief, hope and happiness which came over me as we sat there in the semi-darkness. It was one of the greatest moments in my life. Stepping outside onto the cold, rainy streets of Berlin, I realized how free I was. Free to go. I was going to become a part of the country that had brought so much light to my heart. Right away we started making plans. I remember us making a long to-do list that we had to work through in order to solve everything in the shortest possible period of time.

When we returned to my parents' place, I found myself standing in the kitchen with my father, looking for a way to tell him the news. He somehow knew that I had something important to tell him. I didn't know how to begin so I cautiously told him that I was thinking of moving to Canada and he started crying right away. I was very touched to see that. He put his arms around me and kept on whispering:

"My Pina, my Pina". After his emotions calmed down, he asked me if I was really sure about it and then he wished me all the best on my way. My mother was gone for a couple of days and so my father brought the news to her when she got back. Her reaction was similar to that of my father and for the next weeks, whenever I saw them, they were looking tearful. Yet, they repeatedly said that in view of the number of young, unemployed people around there then, my decision made a lot of sense.

My parents had always told me that, although they could not give us luxury, they had been able to build something very important: a solid basis upon which my sister and I could move on to an even higher step of development. They had both come from a poor background and had been able to lift our family from the lower to the middle class. It seemed that the dimension of my decision was somehow affecting all of us, in the same way that their own departure from Wismar had done, years earlier. They were integrating my departure into the history of the family and I must say that I was proud to be able to break new ground.

Meanwhile Pierre had gone back alone to Canada to make preparations over there. On the last day which I had to organize things in Berlin, my sister came to accompany me. She couldn't believe the determination with which I followed up on my plan. In the metro, she sat opposite me with sad eyes and told me that she was having a hard time dealing with the fact that I was leaving. I was surprised by what she said, for I never knew how much she really cared about me.

In childhood, five years can make a big difference and so we had never had a chance to become real friends. By the time I went into the music business, she was a teenager and had other interests. I secretly admired the way she managed her life. Having friends and being popular was something I had never experienced. She seemed to be able to get whatever she wanted. We all have different ways of dealing with things and I understood that she admired me as much as I admired her. I learned that she had lived through much the same things as I had. The difference was that she had defended her personal space with more success. I'm glad for her.

She told me that she had often felt sorry, seeing her big sister get squeezed by the authoritarian regime at home. She felt our parents had been too busy with my strict education while, although she had had more liberty to do what she wanted, she had been a bit forgotten.

So, only a few days before my departure, after having been apart for a long time, we discovered that there existed a real bond between us. This made us use the few occasions when we had a chance to meet in the years after that, to talk about all the things we had never discussed before. The fact is that we are closer now when we are so far apart than when we lived only two hours away from each other.

Canada, March 1992

Finally, Pierre came back for the last time. We spent the last two days together with my parents in Frankfurt (Oder). As we were already organized, there was nothing much left to do. We left on a Saturday and my parents were there to see us off. Unfortunately Jana was unable to make it. After an emotional goodbye Pierre, Jan and I walked towards the gate. My parents waved to us and I saw their eyes filling with tears again. I smiled at them and after the gate door closed, it was as if I had fully entered the future. When we were seated in the plane, my thoughts turned back to the past. A mad jumble of events raced through my mind and I began to realize the enormity of the step I was taking. As the plane started moving it began to dawn on me just how final this was.

And so to Canada. We arrived in the early evening and the house, which I had such beautiful memories of, was now my home. It was all so wonderful that I was afraid to mess something up. I wanted to be good and make the best out of this chance. The first day after our arrival I started cleaning the house like crazy. I didn't allow myself to sit down since whenever I did, I became restless. My mind was constantly telling me that I needed to prove myself. I was so nervous about losing control and not being on top of things. And of course, I really wanted to please my boyfriend.

In daily life-situations, I found myself hiding behind Pierre. Largely due to language difficulties, I didn't understand much of what was going on around me. Surprisingly, even though I didn't know anyone, everyone who came to the house seemed to know me. Pierre's business was located at home at this time and there were always people coming in and out.

Another strange thing for me was the facility of everything. To be able to turn the heating on at the flick of a switch instead of getting coals from the basement was a big deal. I wasn't used to that anymore. One night Pierre made a phone-call and twenty minutes later someone knocked on our door, bringing a pizza. I couldn't believe it. I didn't know that such things existed. Nor could I comprehend that there was no delivery charge for it either! In my head I automatically asked myself:

"Who allowed that? Doesn't the system nag about so much unnecessary comfort?"

One day I went to Montreal with Pierre and just looking at the high buildings made me feel insecure. I felt like Crocodile Dundee, lost amongst the giant skyscrapers. The only comfortable place was in the car and from there I enjoyed watching the action. Pierre had to go to a business meeting in one of the buildings. Eventually, I decided that I would like a croissant but I had to cross the street to get to the bakery. I got out of the car but the impression of the city was too strong for me. I was afraid. In Berlin, there are no such parts of town. Most of the buildings are limited to about seven stories in height. So I walked once around the car and then got back inside, still hungry.

I had heard so much about crime in big capitalist cities that I was more than a little scared to walk on the street by myself. Later, when I was walking with Pierre, I stared at the people, admiring how self-confidently they moved through the busy sidewalks. I felt everyone was dressed much more modernly than me and I was sure that they all looked my way, noticing my insecurity. It was simular to my experience of entering West Berlin for the first time. I pressed my hand into Pierre's, making sure not to lose track of him. It took me about three trips to the city before my lack of confidence started to give way to excitement.

As far as Jan was concerned we had found a nice lady who agreed to take care of him a few hours a day. He was a little shy at first but I was glad to see how quickly he became friends with her. He picked up the French language incredibly fast and from then on our family communicated in three languages. I was relieved to see that at least Jan seemed to adapt relatively easily to the new surroundings.

Things like answering the telephone, going into shops, ordering pizza, picking up the language and learning to drive were tough for me at first. Shortly before I left Germany I had obtained my driver's license but I had little practical experience and many of the traffic signs in Canada were a complete puzzle to me. There was so much to try and get hold of. It partly explains the difficulties I encountered on the road to learning to live, western-style.

It also complicated our life as a couple. Pierre became impatient because he assumed I was lazy rather than insecure. After a while, our frequent misunderstandings made it hard for us to get along. I got frustrated because Pierre was in charge of everything but there was no choice. I wasn't able to take care of things at that time. His control put me at his mercy and we started to develop an unequal relationship. Pierre felt overloaded with responsibilities and I felt guilt and anger about my inability to adjust fast enough. Just when I thought I had fought my way through to a new life, it seemed to be closing back in on me. I started to feel trapped again.

I remember a feeling of pressure in my neck. The global control of the system over most parts of my life had given me a sort of invisible ring around my neck. Its pressure was an unforgettable reminder, keeping me aware of the fact that I was always being observed. Whether it was from an outside authority or from my parents, I had had to get permission or confirmation for whatever I wanted to do.

Driving in Canada alone in my car, the pressure emerged again and for the first time I was able to identify it. I realized that it was something I had brought with me from my past. I felt the need to turn around to see if there was someone watching over me, controlling me, judging what I was doing. I couldn't quite believe that I was free to go where I wanted. When I wanted to turn left I could do so. When I wanted to go right, that was o.k. as well. And if I didn't feel like going home straight away, I could stop somewhere else, just as I wished. When I would finally arrive home there would not be anyone waiting for me with questions as to what I had done and where I had been.

I had to pinch myself at times, to make sure it was all real. It was an incredible experience to feel that I was in charge but it was only after I was more confident about driving the car. It was not so when I drove the car for the first time alone. On my way I suddenly saw a policeman on the side of the road waving his arm. I immediately thought the worst:

"Oh, no. I don't need a ticket right now. What the heck did I do wrong?"

I pulled the car over and stopped, a little too rapidly of course. Then I had problems getting out of the car. I was so nervous that I didn't realize that my sunscreen was in the way, so I hit my head on it as I got out.

I immediately began to plead with the police officer, asking him to forgive me and let me go, because this was my first time alone driving the car. He replied in French and at that time, I understood none at all. He gave me various signs and pointed towards the roadway. I thought he was trying to explain to me what I had done wrong. When he started laughing I got even more mixed up. He then began to speak English and I finally understood that he was only warning the oncoming traffic about the dangerous ice which was built up on the road. I was free to go back to my car.

In doing so I hit my head again on the sunscreen and I got really upset. I just wanted to get away from this embarrassing situation. Now my car didn't want to move. I looked back and the cop was again trying to show me something. This time it was a little red light on my dash which indicated that the handbrake was still on. Now that was enough! I finally drove away, as carefully as I could. Unexpected ice built up on the road! Who thinks of such things? Well, I was in Canada indeed. That was a funny moment which I can laugh about today. Back then it was a mountain for me which was tough to cross.

I didn't really know what to expect or what was expected of me. Everything was strange and there were many things I couldn't make sense out of at all. I got the wrong impression sometimes because things were so different from that which I had known before. For example, Pierre's relationships with other people constantly surprised me. To me it seemed that he was everybody's best friend. When he spoke to the operator, it sounded to me as though they knew each other. The first time I dialled 'zero', I mentioned that I was Pierre's girlfriend, since I had the impression that there could only be one operator.

I got confused in other ways too. Pierre had tried to describe to me one day, the world of deals and bargains he lived in. I took it very seriously and began to bargain the price of things, inappropriately, at gas stations and grocery stores!

Pierre spoke mainly in French to the people around us, so I understood nothing but the laughter and the fun they seemed to be having. Then I caught on that it wasn't pure friendship I was seeing. Some of these people hardly knew each other. It was the expression of a positive attitude towards life that I was seeing and I was not used to that at all. So I came to the conclusion that people here are more friendly.

I looked up to Pierre and believed him to be the best person there was, someone close to perfection. I wanted nothing more than a harmonious family life and every little problem made me anxious. I was afraid of losing the important precious moments in our life, which we were beginning to build.

During the second week, Pierre and I started working in his office together. I didn't have much working experience at all and now I couldn't even speak the language! When the phone rang my heart jumped and I was too nervous to take the call. Pierre said he would give me a week to get used to it. How could I explain to him that I was not able to do such a simple thing? The pressure was mounting on me and by the beginning of the following week, I still didn't want to take any calls. I was so shy that I once even asked Pierre to leave the room when I was on the phone but that was obviously ridiculous.

Of course I knew before I came to Canada that we were going to work together. But it wasn't clear in my head what it meant to have my lover also being my boss. When my boss gave me rough instructions, I heard my lover shouting at me. When my boss gave me demanding orders, I felt my lover pushing me around. When I looked in the serious eyes of my boss, I saw my lover being unforgiving with me. That was hard to take. I couldn't take it.

I didn't understand what was happening, so I started to be rebellious. Like a child, I provoked, I was stubborn, I closed myself off. I was back in the old situation of my youth. Pierre got more and more irritated because I was apparently not willing to work properly. His increasing anger frustrated me. When I asked questions in order to understand something, he often didn't have the time to explain it properly. We were both very dissatisfied with the situation and didn't know what to do about it. Noone in particular was to blame. Pierre could no longer handle the way I was acting and I was increasingly frustrated not to be able to get a grip on myself. It was almost three months since my arrival in Canada and our life was becoming like a confused mirror image of what it was we were really searching for. It got to the stage where we were having real difficulty getting through a work day together. Pierre's frustration was nearly complete when he thought that his business was going to suffer as well.

Early one morning in June, Pierre came outside to join me on the balcony where I was having a coffee. For a few moments he simply sat beside me, looking off into the distance. Then, without more ado, he asked me:

"Pina, are you a baby or do you have a problem?" Suddenly I had something to focus on. I realized that things were getting to a serious stage. In the back of my mind was the fear that it would not work out. But it had to! There was no going back. I sat there, searching for the answer.

Since my early youth a 'problem' had been something negative and undesirable. For so long, I had been told the problems stemmed from me. I was angry at myself that I was again the one causing all the trouble. So I told Pierre that I must be a baby and that I would grow up from now on.

In the following weeks I tried hard to improve but it seemed we were still caught up in disaster. Virtually everyday, the office work was posing major dilemmas for me but Pierre could not yet see where the difficulty lay. I couldn't really explain it myself. Pierre had given me some time to prove that I was not just a baby but it began to look as though I was not getting anywhere. I finally had to admit that I had a problem. Pierre assured me that he would stand by my side if I got counselling. Things might have been easier if we had shared the responsibility for improving our relationship. Yet, I accepted his point of view because I was the one losing control most of the time.

For several months, there was a period of apparent stability. Pierre and I were both feeling relieved, having a counselor with whom we could share. The therapy enabled me to express myself in a way which I had found impossible at home. My English improved which gave me confidence. I didn't feel as nervous discussing things with my therapist in the calm of his office. Altogether, things seemed to be getting back on an even keel. Instead, in a way in which I could not foresee, they were about to get even worse.

My German driver's license became invalid and I needed to obtain a Canadian permit in its place. I was so busy doing other things that I didn't think about doing it earlier. So, at the end of six months, I lost the symbol of my freedom. Living in the countryside, everything depended more or less on having a car. Now I had to depend on Pierre to take Jan to the kindergarten and that interfered with his schedule. Once again we had an unequal relationship.

At times, the pressure on Pierre became too much for him to accept. He developed a shortness of temper which I could not really understand. It wasn't my desire that he be inconvenienced. I wanted nothing more than to take care of my own affairs and felt that my hands were tied. I worried about Pierre's disapproval. It got to the point that I couldn't ask him to stop at the grocery store for a newspaper. He felt that he was already doing enough providing transport for Jan when he was very busy. He was also looking after our immigration papers and our general welfare. The tension created by all the things going on was causing us both to trip up over simple matters.

So I had to pass the driving test. I had to do a theoretical test first and I took the bus to get there. I arrived at the office full of anxiety. It was of great importance that I pass, yet I was immediately intimidated by my surroundings. The people spoke mostly French and they looked at me with some displeasure when I asked them if they could speak English to me.

I had brought a certified translation of my German license which did not really satisfy the person behind the counter. Her look unsettled me more but I finally went to sit down for the test. As I started to put my answers in the computer, my hands were shaking. I had some difficulty understanding the English phrasing and of course, dictionaries were not allowed. As each answer went in, the result was confirmed and I spent the time hovering between uncertain relief and impending tears.

By the end I was a lather of sweat and sat uncomfortably waiting for the result. When it showed up, telling me that I had missed out by a single point, I sat there stunned. I went outside feeling only anger that I wasn't allowed to try again for another month. All I could think about was the way it would curb my independence. How desperately I wanted to regain control.

My pride made it nearly impossible to accept what had happened. How was I to go home and tell Pierre that he would have to chauffeur us around for another month? I felt like a trapped animal. No matter how much Pierre tried to be supportive, I was the one being most unforgiving with myself. Even though I could understand some things more clearly through therapy, I still didn't know how to control my anger.

For the days and nights following this letdown, I suppressed my growing anger. Finally one evening, I had a big argument with Pierre. As usual, we were discussing where we were at and Pierre said he was tired of talking about what he considered to be my problems. He told me I should take it all to my therapist, whose job it was to do something about it. I had heard it all before and it seemed as if I wanted to make up for all the time in my life when I was not allowed to talk about myself. If I felt that I was being blocked in any way or if I was told that I was the problem, I lost control.

That night I couldn't stand the rejection anymore. I felt as if it was going to kill me. I ran crying out of the house in my bare feet. I stood shivering in the darkness for a while, until it was no longer possible to remain standing in the snow.

I went back inside the house and thought that Pierre, because he was acting normally, was choosing to ignore me. I became afraid of myself and I struggled with the idea that I might be crazy. I started to scream and hit the walls. I shouted out in German:

"*Ich will nicht sterben. Ich möchte mich doch nur ein bisschen freuen.*"

"I don't want to die. I just want a little happiness." I screamed and screamed. I must have been hysterical. I cried out for my mother and I repeated several phrases over and over:

"Ich hab' doch gar nichts gemacht. Ich bin lieb, ich bin ein liebes Mädchen. Ich versteh' nicht."

"I didn't do anything bad. I am good, I am a good girl. I don't understand." Pierre didn't know what to do either. Things were really out of control. Eventually, he had to call an ambulance. I was in the bedroom, in a cold sweat. I didn't know what I wanted but I didn't want this. Slowly I began to regain control.

Soon I was feeling embarrassed and I went to hide in the darkness of the bathroom. A voice I didn't recognize suddenly started asking me questions. How did I feel? I would have done anything at that moment to get better and save myself and my family from all that trouble. I suppose they could see that I was no longer dangerously excited. I followed the person to the door and was asked to lie down on a stretcher. Even as I was carried outside into the ambulance, I still couldn't understand what was going wrong. I looked at my little boy in Pierre's arms and both of them kissed me goodbye. Why couldn't I have a normal family life? Why all this drama?

Lying in the ambulance I stared at the ceiling and saw only the fragments of my broken dreams. In both my head and heart, one idea resounded:

"You're a failure, Pina, a failure." I wondered if I could get any lower. Had I finally proven to myself that I was never going to make it? I did not want my family to suffer. I had to find a solution but where was I supposed to look for the answer?

The outside help that we had sought was very confusing. The conclusions varied from an extreme PMS syndrome, to a repressed childhood trauma to the twin possibilities that I could be schizophrenic or maniaco depressif. Not only was all this input giving me a more negative self-image, I thought that was where I had to look for an answer. Since I couldn't see or identify this enemy, it scared the hell out of me. For a short time, I actually experienced a kind of relief when I believed that the answer lay in being a maniaco depressif. It was as if I finally had an excuse for losing control.

In the hospital I had a chance to let the pressure go down. It was a break that I badly needed and I passed the time sleeping, thinking and eating. I even spent some time writing lyrics for my album. There was one thought I couldn't escape from. I couldn't figure out my own personal guilt or innocence. Certainly I focused on the guilt. I was afraid to discover the truth about myself, afraid to find out that the problem was in me, just as I had always been taught. I felt as if I was walking through an unknown territory with a black bandage over my eyes. I was terrified that I might fall into a big black hole instead of finding a sunny place where I could rest and live in peace.

I realized that my behavior patterns were similar to when I was a child, the only difference being that my reactions were getting stronger and stronger. I still doubted that the way I had been brought up could have anything to do with my trouble. My parents had always warned me about putting any blame on them. So I was almost ready to accept that I might have a mental disease. I even informed my parents about that possibility, to assure them that I was not going to blame them for anything.

Nonetheless, I decided to make one more attempt to communicate with my parents about the things that had happened during my childhood. I said to myself that if it didn't work this time, then that letter would be my last attempt to have them talk to me about that subject. I would no longer try to get their attention. In the letter I revealed much about the way I felt whilst trying, at the same time, to avoid having it sound like an accusation.

I asked them if they knew of anything that could help to explain my state of mind. Further I asked them if there had ever been a case of mental disease in our family's history which could help me in my present need for a clear diagnosis.

Back home from the hospital, I was welcomed with a lot of love and confidence that our family was going to win this battle together. A couple of weeks after that, I received my parents' answer. I remember my hands trembled as I unfolded the paper. Somehow I felt this could mean so much to me. The first sentences told me that I had not been heard at all. I kept on reading and the tears started rolling down my cheeks.

They said that my letter had made them very unhappy but they expressed their hope that my health would never become a serious problem in my life. They were surprised that I had to go into medical care. It was another bitter pill of reality they would have to swallow. They pointed out that I was brought up in a simple and harmonious family and that they could not understand why I should feel the way I had described it to them. And yes, five generations ago there had been a single case of psychiatric disease. They ended their letter with the hope that the information would be of help and the advice that I needed to become stronger in life.

I had to face the fact that my parents were still unable to understand me. It was just as it had always been. My thoughts and feelings had always been unjustified in their opinion. Why should it be any different now?

It also made me realize where my actual feelings of rejection and of being misunderstood came from. It was a confirmation of the things that I remembered thinking in my childhood. Whilst at times I wasn't sure if my memory was clear, this letter confirmed just how close all those memories were to reality. Even though it caused me incredible pain, it somehow gave me strength at the same time. I felt closer to the root of my anger and therefore closer to its resolution.

As far as my driver's license was concerned, it wasn't even over when I finally passed the theory test, the second time around. The same thing happened with the practical test. I failed and for a while, I was still devastated.

Yet, something began to change inside of me. I thought to myself that things could only get better and decided to seek what I needed without being afraid of other people's opinion. I began to discover that the fear of being controlled and judged was my real enemy. Now I had something to base my self defense strategy on. The truth is never far behind, yet sometimes so hard to discover.

I dropped my worries about Pierre's impatience towards my 'slow' progress and decided to become my own best friend.

After four months of nearly constant struggle, I finally got my Canadian driver's license. I had stopped seeing the psychologist because I was not sure if I was really in good hands after all that had happened to us. During that time, a person came into my life who offered me a great deal of comfort and enlightenment. She was somebody who had been through a similar emotional experience and we were able to share a lot. Her experience enabled her to really help me understand many things about the forgotten heart of a child and about ways of learning to forgive and how to reduce the pain that sometimes seems to be sending us mad.

Up until then, Pierre was the only person I knew well enough to share a deep conversation with. It was healthy for both of us that I had found a friend to talk to. It removed a lot of the pressure from our relationship as a couple. The same thing was true for Jan, since it was important for him as well to build connections to new friends. He had made a couple of good friends at his daycare, whom he invited to our place to play. From here on things improved but it seemed as if we were still dragging some bad memories around with us. We often found ourselves stumbling over them when we didn't expect it. So now we had to face a new challenge, to completely let go of the past.

In Canada, I was confronted with a world which was very different from the one I had known. It was as if I had to learn every step from the beginning. There were always new surprises waiting for me, as to how things were handled here. I remember how astonished I was buying groceries in a store. When they put my articles in a bag for me, I stood by, not knowing what to do. In Germany, the cashiers don't even look at the customer and they sling your food down the metal ramp it hits the barrier at the end. At the same time, you are expected to say a friendly '*Danke*'. If you're not fast enough packing the food in the grocery bags, then other people's goods come rushing down the ramp with a speed that threatens to push yours onto the floor. In Canada, the cashiers greeted me with a smile and there was someone else to put the shopping into a bag. It made a big difference.

I did not expect to have a new life magically free of problems or difficulties but I did come here with a great deal of hope. I hoped that I would find my own way without being supervised by anybody else. I needed a chance to try it alone, to prove to myself that I could do it, without constantly being checked up on, as I had been in the old Germany. Up until now I can say that I have succeeded and that success has allowed me to grow and develop self-confidence. I am stronger in many ways and also emotionally wiser. I had a chance to do so before my new environment got hold of me, possibly wanting to interfere with my life. I had enough time to built my true inner grounds based on my individuality before outside factors could eventually throw me off the chair, as they used to.

Sometimes I came close to being knocked off balance, especially within my relationship with Pierre. Still, I managed to find an open road towards my self belief and keep on it. I had to leave the past behind not only in words but also by freeing my heart from the negative memories that I still dragged around with me. My creative work is an important part of this process, since it allows me to review my life freely and to clear my head from uncertainty. I am able to express myself at will. That is partly because of the simple fact that, in western society, I am allowed to do so but most of all, it is because I have a better understanding of my life. That is actually what enables me to talk now.

The confusion I had for so long lived in, made me keep my mouth closed. I literally did not know what words to use to start a sentence. For a long time, I did not even try. After overcoming that period of silence, I started to write lyrics. From that point, I was ready to face the real beginning of my artistic career. I can see now how the past years have been a preparation for all of this. The confusion that I felt in the adaptation process has vanished and is now being replaced with a new clarity about what it is I want and where I am going. Canada has become my home and the thing which has guided me most through the period of adjustment, is a little word called *hope*.

> *"Go ahead, start to live . . . . .*
> *Go ahead, start to fly . . . . .*
> *Hate and anger you don't deserve.*
> *Hate and anger make it hard to find*
> *what we really need.*
> *It is called wisdom,*
> *love and wisdom."*

Christmas in Germany, 1994

What can I do to change the situation between my parents and myself for the better? Does it need a change? I certainly don't feel like hearing the same old stories again. I feel it is my turn to express to them exactly what I have in my heart. Yet I have doubts. Is it really so important for me to get my message through? After having tried so much to improve the understanding between us, perhaps it's better to just let it be. In any case, although I am uncertain of what may happen, Jan and I are going home for Christmas.

After three years in Canada, I find myself standing on that same balcony in that same apartment I know so well. It still faces the building that my parents used to work in, although now it contains the administration offices of another department. I ask my father how it feels to face that building every day after all that has happened in the past few years. He answers that he is partly glad that it is all over, especially the long shifts and the incredible responsibility that was tied to his job. He now enjoys coming home from work and being there for nobody else but himself and his wife. He also expresses disappointment towards the people who treat him and the now defunct Security organization with contempt. He feels he honestly worked hard to protect a state that was, in many respects, doing them good.

I remember a summer night in 1989, shortly after the wall came down. I was sitting with my parents out on the balcony when a person walking on the street started calling us names, expressing his contempt for the Secret Service. It was common knowledge that our apartment building was for members of the organization. My father could not take that kind of humiliation and ran outside to chase the guy. I can still see the sorrowful face of my mother who knew only too well her husband's limitless anger.

I felt really sorry for what my parents had to go through then. It was as if they were caught in a timewarp and still had to pay for the positions they had once held. I left the house at a run, to search for my father. I knew his rage couldn't be trusted. I eventually found him walking alone, having lost track of his persecutor. I was relieved because it would only have made things worse had he found him. We walked back home together.

There had already been much more trouble than that. Before the dismantlement of the Stasi organization, people from all over the city came to demonstrate on the street outside our apartment block. There was a stream of people, many hundreds strong, marching with lighted candles in their hands. They carried placards and there were occasional shouts of 'Stasi out!'. They were mainly peaceful but it was obvious that the organization and its role in upholding the state, had left many people embittered.

Verbal provocation on the streets did not stop but slowly, my father's attitude changed. My mother told me about a day when my father was painting the balcony. As he stood on the ladder, somebody passed and called up to him:

"What do you care about your balcony?! All of you are soon going to be put in jail anyway." There was hatred in those words, yet my father replied with nothing but a confident smile. That was in the summer of 1994. Many of the former Stasi members have moved out of the block. Some of them were looking for a new beginning, seeking for a place where nobody but themselves knew where they came from. No doubt some just wanted to get away from the difficulties caused by being in that place. It was like a place on a map that was marked by a large black X.

Despite all of that, my parents still live in the same place today. It is no surprise to me. When I ask them about the possibility of moving away, they reply no, they are not in a rush to leave the place where they have spent most of their lives. They feel they have nothing to be ashamed of and no reason to run away. My father does not feel like leaving the nice apartment he has renovated with considerable effort. He feels a strong need to hold on to what he's got in his private life, after having lost so much in his professional life. Every item in their apartment is an expression of love and pride about what they have achieved. Right now their greatest hope is to keep the jobs they have. It isn't easy to get one, especially for people of their age and background.

My mother had a secretarial career so she had a better chance of getting a new start. My father's experience was more limited. After a long period of unemployment, he now works for a company which is clearing the defunct military depots and firing ranges of the Russian army, as well as looking for bombs that still remain from the Second World War.

At the moment, my parents' only goal is to have a regular income so as to be able to keep up with a modest but relatively comfortable life style. For the first time in their lives they are enjoying a normal schedule without the intense pressure they used to have. One of the ironies of life for them has been that through all the years of hard work for the GDR, they were never able to get the garden they had always dreamed about. Now, after the wall has come down, they have realized that dream.

The process of improving social conditions in Germany is a long one but things are slowly getting better. For example, many of the eastern papers and diplomas which were not valid at first, are now being accepted. Many East Germans were thoroughly discouraged by such moves in the beginning and it did not help the process of reunification. It was also obvious that the government could not afford to put such a vast number of people back into school. Another positive sign that things are improving is that the value of the Deutschmark has increased quite a lot. One of the most interesting features of the new Germany is that the old East, which in 1989 had very outdated infrastructure, is now being supplied with the very latest and most sophisticated equipment. It is a curious thing to witness the transformation from the outmoded to leading-edge technology in shopping centers, offices, banks and so on. For my parents, there is a certain new pride beginning to take shape as the changes become more tangible. But the past is still with us.

Three years of living in another country has enabled me to let go of much of the anxiety my father's behavior caused me. I was determined to hang on to this new freedom and never again to accept such a situation. Yet, at Christmas, it happened again.

Late one evening, on the fifth day of our stay, my mother opened a drawer to get something and a pile of papers fell out and went flying all over the place. Instead of just gathering the stuff up and accepting that things like that happen, my father began to pick on me. As he started to clean up the mess, he began to raise his voice, complaining loudly and passionately about me and my strange approach towards life.

It was like old times, when he would use any occasion to jump on me, no matter if I was actually involved or not. My heart would crunch inside me and I would hope for a quick end to his anger. Oh, how much do I know and deeply hate this kind of situation. I felt as if invisible floodgates, which had long been holding back a huge weight, had suddenly opened and there was nothing that could stop the outrush of energy to come. Before my father knew what was happening, I jumped at him like a tiger and even surprised myself by the force of my emotions, as I gave him the wildest speech of my life. In effect, I was laying down a kind of bottom line to him. It went like this:

"Do not talk to me if you have neither respect nor good intentions and do not even take my name in your mouth when you don't even know what is really bothering you. Now it is my turn to tell you that you have always used me as your anger-garbage-explosion center and I have had enough of it! You were able to lead your life because you had me to spit out your frustration upon. Now I am carrying the anger that you put into me and I have to do the job you were supposed to do yourself: anger-management. Yet you stand there judging me and my problems, always telling me how well you have managed compared to me. You have no reason to feel a better or more worthy human being than I am. You were never able to look honestly and clearly at yourself. You simply transferred your problems to me. This was unfair and abusive to start with. I was a child who depended on you and who had trusted to your love. I have for so long carried a pack-sack full of guilt and been unable to believe in myself. This is what really caused the problems that you interpreted as being the fault of my weak nature.

This has been burning inside of me for a long time and you have never taken me seriously enough to bother to listen. When I said:

"I hurt," you replied:

"You don't hurt." When I said:

"I need friends," you answered:

"You don't need friends, everybody is corrupt and they are no good for your development." When I said:

"I am strong," you said:

"You are the weakest person I have ever known." All of this ignorance and humiliation has come today to return to its roots; to *you father*."

My mother said more or less nothing and went to hide in a back room. I decided to go for a walk. For the first time I did not care what my father was thinking of me or whether or not he was hurting. I strongly believed it was my turn to express what I felt after having carried so many scars around with me for so long. If there had been perhaps one solitary word from them in the past, to express the notion that maybe, just maybe, they had not always been perfectly, one hundred per cent right, I might never have uttered a word of such a speech. I can forgive everything and anything that they did or didn't do because I know that we all make mistakes. What I cannot forgive is to hear them repeat how perfect they are and how all problems are related to me and only me.

After I got back from my walk, I could see that my father was very nervous. He began to defend himself, saying that my behavior was impossible. Although I was very well aware of that, I decided to turn up the temperature some more. I was not willing to let it come to this kind of situation a second time. I was determined to let it out now, once and for all. I let nothing he said pass without relating my behavior to the attitude he had had towards me in all those past years. I told him:

"I will get as impossible as I have to, in order to make you listen for once, to what I have to say. I will not stop until everything I need to say is said. You have never learned the language of respectful communication and here is your pay. I will scream out the message at the top of my lungs until you hear it. It is my turn to preach and your turn to listen. Here you see my killer eyes that you have glared at me with so many times, here you get the anger that you put on me when I had nowhere to hide. I am giving all of it back to you, as my health and sanity demands. Never, ever again will you make the smallest attempt to put me down. Respect me and I will respect you. For now you deserve only these expressive finger signs. So stay where you are and listen to what I have to say and to show to you. You will not intimidate me anymore. From now on you will receive from me only what you give. If you had granted me any understanding ever, I would be able to do the same for you. I am your mirror. I am the product of your education. If you want to continue to deny your mistakes, that's up to you. In the past you have heard many compliments for the good parts and that is the only thing you were ever willing to accept. This is the first time I am concentrating on the negative things which stand between us and won't allow us to have a good time together. I for my part will not walk away from here without having told you about your weaknesses for a change."

As soon as he started to be angry I was there to show him even more anger. I insisted on him witnessing what it feels like to be overwhelmed with blame, criticism and anger. At times I used English sentences so he would feel the same thing as I had when he yelled words I couldn't really understand because I was too little. Any attempt he made to talk back to me, I cut off with domination and authority, just as he had done to me. The torture of my heart ended in these two hours of confrontation. My mother whispered to me that it was enough now, that father had gotten the message. She whispered that I had to understand that he felt very humiliated and that I shouldn't push it further since he had begun to cry. I could see for myself that the limit had been reached but forbade my heart to cry out for the feelings of my father.

They were ready to talk. I said:

"To talk is all I ever wanted." The three of us sat down in the living room and began a calm conversation. For the first time I felt my parents open to what I was going to say. I started crying when I told them that I wished that politics hadn't played such an important role in our family life. I let them know all about the difficulties I had had, in integrating into different groups because of my socialist convictions. I had only wanted to please my parents, so I had done everything I possibly could to behave as they expected me to. My father now said that he hadn't expected me to fight for politics in that way but I had to remind him of the daily lectures in which he blamed me for not expressing my political attitude strongly enough. My father wept that it was unfair and not the right moment for that kind of scene. I told him I agreed utterly with him and then asked him:

"When did you ever choose the right time? Where are your regrets for having destroyed so many vacations, family parties and weekends with your limitless anger?" He said that the past was the past and that he couldn't change it. I argued that he had been much older than I was now when he had hurt his family so, that politics had counted far more than the hearts of his own children. My mother agreed to most of the things I said, which amazed me. I continued. I told him about my sadness at being made responsible for every conceivable problem including his high blood pressure and his grey hair. Many of the things I brought up he simply could not remember and thought I might be making them up. However, my mother supported me once again by asking my father to allow me to express what it was that weighed so heavily on my heart. Obviously my father began to feel attacked from two sides. The discussion started slowly to heat up again since my father was unable to repress his anger about the degradation he felt at the tongue-lashing I had given him. Yet, everything he said only confirmed my complaints. Even his inability to keep the discussion calm was a proof of what I was saying. He began to speak louder and louder and said that it would be my fault if he and my mother divorced. At this point my mother interjected:

"You are doing it again! Again you are putting the guilt on Pina."

My father started to act as if he was caught in a trap. This was the end of any calm discussion. I was surely finished with what I had to say and saw no reason to start out another time. My father's specialty is not to work things out completely. They stay unresolved and therefore always come back again sooner or later. He could blame me as much as he wanted to, regarding my behavior. By his attitude, he was proving himself wrong. He doesn't like to have a serious confrontation like that, accept when it is created by him. He likes to be the one loading the guns.

At that moment he could not accept what had happened at all and told me to go and sleep at my grandma's place. I could understand his reaction and went out for a long walk again to give things a chance to cool off. I considered going back to Canada before the planned departure date, if we were not able to get things under control. It was a great feeling to know that I wasn't stuck there, that I had my own life to go back to.

Outside I took several deep breaths. Little Pina had finally stood up against the angry authority of her father. The same father who, though he carries much love in his heart, has always expected his family to jump up and down with his radical emotions. The relief I felt at that moment is hard to describe; I felt as light as a feather. It was as if I had shaken off a tightly-fitting shell and I now felt supple and free and strong. How could I have stood up against the angry words of my father if I had not decided to act in my own best interests?

The different kind of life that I had discovered far away from him, had shown me the truth. He really had been practicing emotional abuse by directing his terrifying anger at me and never listening to what I wanted to say. From the moment when my mother had dropped the papers on the floor and my father had begun to get up steam in the same old way, I knew I could not accept a further verbal attack from him.

What I could no longer do was to return home with that piercing feeling in my belly which made it so hard for me to be loving and happy with myself. Under the circumstances it could have meant not having any further contact with them in the future. I could have simply added my name to the list of people whom my parents no longer frequented or should I say, vice versa. Yet I was their daughter. Surely it could not come to that for me as well?

It had made me very happy to see my mother admitting to the things I had brought up in front of my father. I believed that she was finally ready to speak the truth about the past, openly. I was all the more disappointed the next morning when she seemed to have changed her mind. Almost the first thing she said to me was:

"In the end, everything is your fault, Pina." I was not going to let either of them get away with that again. I pushed her away, saying:

"Go to that abominable father of mine and continue being his accomplice if you will. Just yesterday you managed to openly admit the truth for the first time and today your words have turned themselves around. I don't need you people and I don't want to see you until you decide to stand by my side! I have spent my life coping with your feelings and your situations and since, for years, you have never considered mine, I see no reason to support you now. The time of being unconditionally obedient to your point of view is over."

During the following two days, I spent a lot of time with Jan at my grandma's place. She could very well understand what the confrontation was all about. She tried to make me feel better by saying that it had always been like that and that things would get back in order very soon. I explained to her that it was exactly this pattern of terrible war and golden peace which concerned me most. Living in Canada had given me the chance to break free of what I had discovered to be an unhealthy way of dealing with one another. I told her that the old ways, of things sorting themselves out over time but never getting resolved, were finished for me. I suppose that, at her age, she could hardly dream that things were suddenly going to improve now.

When I came back to my parents' place, we slowly began family talk, just as in old times. When it was almost time for bed, my father stayed seated on the couch and I felt that he wanted to talk. It was the night before my birthday and for the first time, we had a really good conversation. Both of us made big efforts to keep it free of the former judgements and accusations. Instead we showed sincere interest about what each other had to say. How can one explain that sudden turn of fate? My father said that it was important to him to talk, especially before my birthday. I appreciated that very much. He said that he wished a conversation like this might have happened a long time before. I told him that the letter I had sent from Canada had been one of my serious attempts to start the communication but that their answer had been true to their old stance. I had more or less given up the hope of ever having my parents comprehend the simplest thing about me.

Returning briefly to the wild scenes of a few days ago, he wondered whether or not my complaints were completely justified. I told him I had no reason to make things up because I was searching for peace, not striving to make things worse. In any case, I said, I didn't think it possible that our personal situation could have deteriorated further and that is why I had finally spoken from the heart, with no holds barred. Everything I had put on the table had come from deep within me, where it had been buried for many years. I tried to show him that it was all the emotional flotsam and jetsam that was lying around from the shipwreck of our unmanageable relationship. It wasn't there by accident.

My father said that for many years, they had found me to be a stranger; unreachable and uncommunicative. To that I replied:

"What you are saying about me is the same way I felt about you." I told him about my feelings as a teenager, when he had been more of a politician to me than a father. I tried to explain how difficult, how next to impossible it had been, to never have a papa to talk to, just a figurehead from whom I received lengthy diatribes. How could I not close myself off? Whose responsibility had it been in those years to encourage a trusting relationship between parents and children?

Besides, I went on, I had tried many times to talk privately but he had always managed to turn any little talk at all, into a political one. The smallest matter had always been elevated to the ideological plane within minutes. I had been forced to live on a platform where I could feel nothing emotionally and understand very little. In order to protect myself from that I stopped asking things altogether. I stopped talking about myself or my problems and concerns. I repressed everything for fear of having it held up to the stark light of the socialist day. My father tried to justify himself by saying that I was a hard nut to crack. I asked him what the hell he felt the need to crack me for?! A human being is not a nut to be cracked and it was only natural for me to grow my shell thicker and thicker as a protection.

I had felt let down without reason. I had been a fine girl and a model student and I had worked hard to achieve that status. I had great marks in school and filled my free time by reading books and singing in the choir. I had had an innocent life as a teenager because I had always tried to please my parents by not developing friendships, just as they had advised me. How would you have dealt, I asked him, with those teenagers who smoked, who listened to loud music or who hung out with their friends until late at night? As I know now, those were the teenagers who had the more normal life. Had you allowed me to be a bit more like them, I would never have become as rebellious as you found me to be.

You made life hard for us all by teaching me not to communicate and to keep my personal feelings and opinions hidden. When I wanted to talk about myself you always asked me what for, as if it could be of no earthly use. How could you expect me to suddenly have trusting conversations with you. Children are the reflection of their parents. You were my leader and I became as you educated me to be. You find it very natural to accept congratulations for the good results and success of your child. Yet when it comes to my mistakes you reject any responsibility for it. If you would accept me the way I am there would be no reason for rebellion.We would have no scenes such as we have so often known. I carried your mistakes along with my own, which made me believe that I was full of mistakes whilst you had none. Any child who is made to feel that way can not be happy. Today is the first time we are having a balanced conversation and it feels incredibly good.

My father tried to explain his tough approach to education by the nature of his job. He said that the former enemy of socialism had been trying to seduce young people especially, to make them turn against the system. He had been ordered to pay special attention to my education so that no bad influences could possibly reach me. I was perfectly satisfied with that explanation. All I had ever wanted was to have parents I could talk to. I just wanted things to make sense. Instead, I had felt squeezed until I could no longer breathe and I had just started hitting out at things around me. When that would happen, my parents would stop and innocently ask:

"What's the matter with you, how can one lose control like that?" It drove me crazy. Now my father tried to hold my sister up to me as a good example. He had done that in the past, insisting that she had had the same conditions. However, I could now point out that it had been possible for her to learn from my mistakes. Maybe she had realized that my approach hadn't been the good one. The younger ones take natural advantage of the road that their elders have opened up ahead of them and that is o.k. I just wanted him to acknowledge that and stop saying that she was better. Besides she told me about some serious confrontations she had had, that were never mentioned. I saw her in similar situations to me and he did not react the same way at all the second time around. It was not only Jana who made the difference. Father had obviously made the choice of the favorite one. I asked him:

"Can't you see that by reminding me often in the past and even today of how much better Jana is in your opinion, that you are hurting me unfairly? That is your way of judging many things without thinking of the consequences and those are that I did not have a chance to believe that you truly love me. With that disbelief I would of course rebel against you and your rejection of me."

When my father expressed his concern for the way I acted, he reproached me especially for doing it at my age and state of development. I had to remind him that he had behaved no less badly when he was many years older than I was and therefore supposed to be even more experienced. I told him:

"I have only put a mirror in your face and let you know that I have learned all these things from you. It was no more than what you have done to me over the years without once saying 'I'm sorry'. I demonstrated an exchange of roles because there was no other way left to make you understand. Countless times I was instructed by you to accept life and not to put the blame on others. I have simply turned it around and made you see that you were actually doing and teaching me the things that you now criticize in me. In my own life, I am already handling confrontations differently and it has cost me a lot of effort to break free. It is not so that we grow up and suddenly don't react anymore. I felt the need to show you once what you left up to me to deal with by having exposed me for so long to your verbal abuse. Since you have put politics in my face so often during family conversations, I will do that now to you also. Your behavior and attitude is like that of all the officials you worked with. You had no respect for the people of East Germany in general, or for me in particular. It is no wonder that they turned their back on you and a society that left them with no more than the freedom to follow your instructions or to be followed by the Secret Service."

For the first time in my life, my father allowed my words to flow without interrupting or constantly contradicting them. Things seemed to have worked out just fine when he suddenly said:

"Pina, if you don't excuse yourself for your behavior the other day I see no reason to visit you in the future. I would feel too humiliated and not able to get along with you." My answer was immediate:

"Well, Father, I have considered the same thing from my side after I believed that I hadn't gotten the message through. Tonight we have had a very open and calm discussion. What was the use to go through all that effort if not for the sake of our relationship. If the conclusion you have come to is that we should not see each other anymore, then we need not have bothered to make any effort to resolve our problems. Besides, I am still convinced that my action of the other evening was necessary. How do you otherwise explain that we are sitting here in the living room for the first time talking about nothing but ourselves?"

Then the last thing he needed to ask me was:

"The other night. Did it have anything to do with your disease, Pina?" What a welcome opportunity for me to tell him:

"This is the end of my disease, papa." I felt such a peace in my heart as I have never felt before when sitting beside my father. Before going to bed we hugged each other and the warmth that lay in that embrace washed away all the bad memories of our past.

The next morning I was received by my parents and Jan with flowers for my birthday and they had put on Pierre's music as a symbol of his presence. We spent the most beautiful day together but something else was different. It took me a little while to figure out that it was the general atmosphere which had changed. It felt light and friendly. Besides all the surprises and presents I got, this was the nicest gift but then, on top of that, something even more wonderful occurred. We went to pick up my grandma and after having cake and coffee together, I took out my father's old guitar which he hadn't touched since the wall had come down. For several years, he had refused to play any music at all. I began to play a song by Nana Mouskouri that all of us knew and everyone started to sing along. Then I decided to play the song my parents used to love to sing together. It was the song that I connect such happy memories with, from the time when my parents gave us their duets. When they heard that, they looked at each other and began to sing, as in years past. I could see the tears coming up in their eyes and I knew that my nicest birthday present was yet to come.

Silently I prayed for my father to take the guitar and was as excited as a little kid when he really did. In the beginning, he was a bit shy because he hadn't played an instrument for so long but then, with the volume slowly increasing, he began to recover his memory of the songs that seemed to have been lost forever. My grandma got into the action as well and insisted that I go and find her the harmonica which was somewhere in the house. And here we were giving the concert of our lives, with all the talent and fire that had been sleeping for so long. It was funny to see this family of ours waking up like that. It was as if we were really indestructible, as if the long years of hardship had been a sort of strange hibernation we had had to go through.

The party went on the next day because it was Silvester night. My father had bought some rockets and other noisy articles to celebrate this event. Jan's particular goal was not to go to sleep under any circumstances. He insisted on staying up until it was twelve o'clock. Meanwhile he walked around with his watch to make sure he wouldn't miss it. My mother had prepared a delicious fish meal which is a tradition in our region on the night before New Year. Then my mother wanted all of us to say hello to the neighbors. I can remember when I was little, we often celebrated events together but this had stopped many years since. I was so happy to see my parents open up again to the things they used to enjoy so much and which they had so long neglected. The neighbors were very happy to see us and surprised at the sudden change in my parents. Even though my father was a little awkward still, my mother enjoyed herself abundantly and even tried to smoke. What a surprise for my father! I had to laugh to see him sitting there a little stiff, as if he had to check out first if it was o.k. to let go.

His favorite occupation on that day was to fire the rockets and fortunately for him, he had his grandson there as an excuse for him to indulge in some fireworks! In previous years, he had not felt comfortable doing it by himself. Now he went outside with Jan early, to shoot a first rocket since, of course, they needed to test whether or not they were working.

As midnight was approaching, I found my parents turning up the volume of the music very high and dancing in an exuberant way together. There was something contagious about that night, some kind of magical happiness in which noone could refuse to join. I did not want to spend time thinking about what might have caused this change in our hearts, maybe it has always been there and just needed to be lived. So I took my little boy and swung with him through the living room.

We welcomed the New Year with big smiles on our faces and a voice of our own: Let's go for it! Outside many of the neighbors, especially the young people, came together to share in the fireworks. My father had not been the only one struck down by the changes. There were many of his age group that had not yet regained the fire for life. To see him there in the middle of the action confirmed just how willing he was to face life with its new challenges and equally new pleasures. Jan jumped up and down excitedly and clapped his hands. Smoke from the fireworks began to fill the street and my mother told me this was the first big fireworks display since the dramatic changes in 1989. We were not alone to greet the New Year with enthusiasm and new hopes. The consciousness of many of those who had been paralyzed by the overwhelming nature of events, was coming alive again. Each rocket was like a symbol, a message from the person who sent it high into the sky:

"That's where we belong and that's where we are going."

fini

ABOUT THE CO-WRITER:

Owen Hughes is a free-lance writer who was born in Sydney, Australia. He has traveled through Europe and North America and lived for extended periods in France and the U.K. He now lives in the Laurentian Mountains of Quebec, Canada with his French-Canadian wife and their three children.